PASTA MACHINE
Cookbook
2021

RECIPES FOR EVERY OCCASION
TO MAKE AT HOME

All rights reserved.
The content contained within this book may not be reproduced, duplicated or transmitted without direct written permission from the author or the publisher.
Under no circumstances will any blame or legal responsibility be held against the publisher, or author, for any damages, reparation, or monetary loss due to the information contained within this book.
Either directly or indirectly.
Legal Notice.
This book is copyright protected.
This book is only for personal use. You cannot amend, distribute, sell, use, quote or paraphrase any part, or the content within this book, without the consent of the author or publisher.
Disclaimer Notice.
Please note the information contained within this document is for educational and entertainment purposes only.
All effort has been executed to present accurate, up to date, and reliable, complete information. No warranties of any kind are declared or implied.
Readers acknowledge that the author is not engaging in the rendering of legal, financial, medical or professional advice.
The content within this book has been derived from various sources. Please consult a licensed professional before attempting any techniques outlined in this book.
By reading this document, the reader agrees that under no circumstances is the author responsible for any losses, direct or indirect, which are incurred as a result of the use of information contained within this document, including, but not limited to, errors, omissions, or inaccuracies.

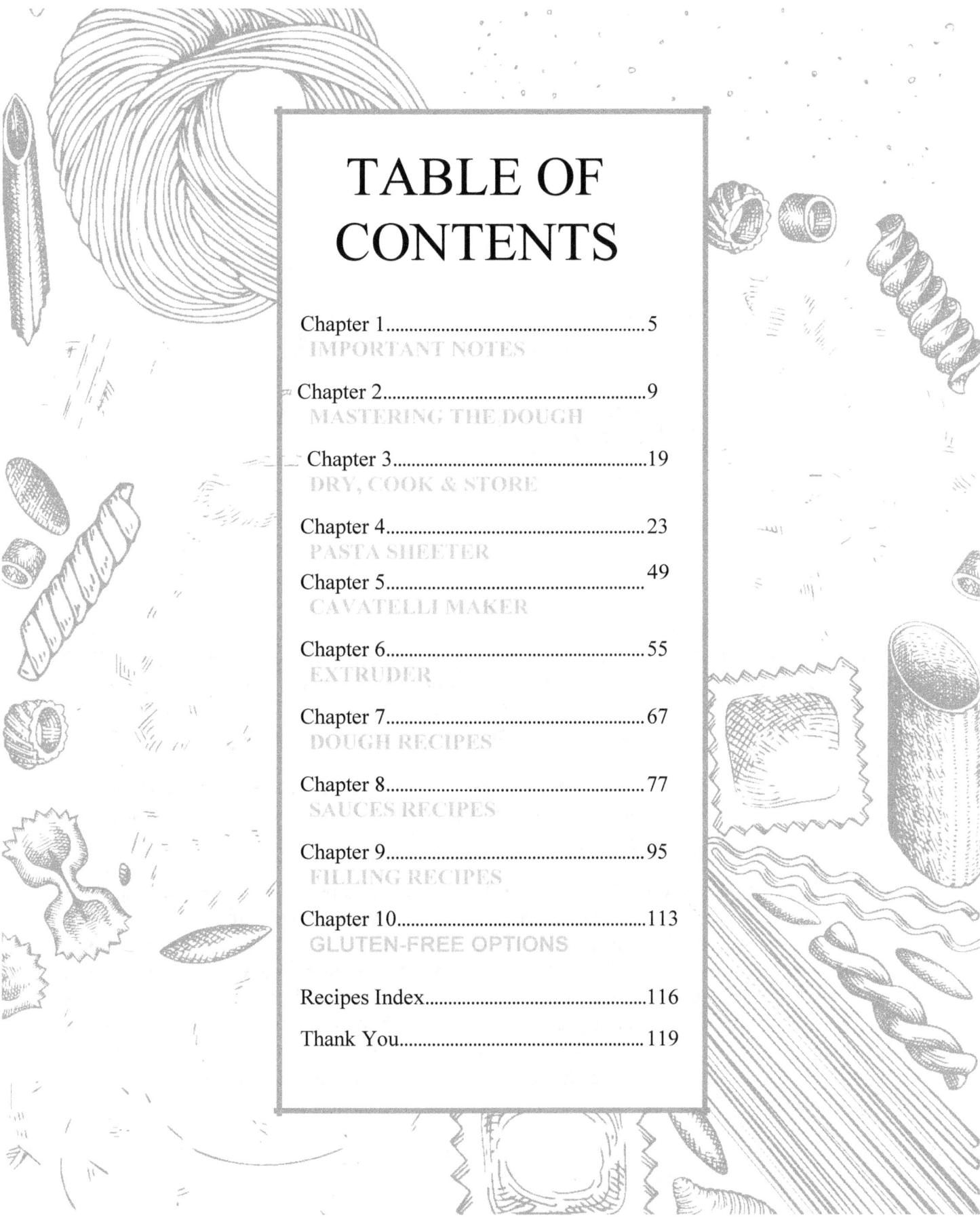

TABLE OF CONTENTS

Chapter 1 5
IMPORTANT NOTES

Chapter 2 9
MASTERING THE DOUGH

Chapter 3 19
DRY, COOK & STORE

Chapter 4 23
PASTA SHEETER

Chapter 5 49
CAVATELLI MAKER

Chapter 6 55
EXTRUDER

Chapter 7 67
DOUGH RECIPES

Chapter 8 77
SAUCES RECIPES

Chapter 9 95
FILLING RECIPES

Chapter 10 113
GLUTEN-FREE OPTIONS

Recipes Index 116

Thank You 119

1. IMPORTANT NOTES

HOW TO USE THIS BOOK
All the recipes are full of flavors, easy and quick to make. This book is been structured to let you be creative and contains full of flavors, easy, and quick recipes. You choose the dough, the pasta shape, the filling, and the sauce to make your own signature dish. You can mix and match the doughs, fillings, and sauces for (almost) an infinite number of tasty possibilities.

I put down some suggestions and recommendations here and there, but I want to leave you the pleasure of discovering many possibilities!

QUANTITY Except where specified, most dough and filling recipes in this book serve four while the sauces serve six. I give you three good reasons for this discrepancy. One, I often end up eating half of the sauce with bread while cooking. Two, often someone at the table would like to soak up some more with a piece of bread. Last but not least, it is always handy to have some tasty homemade sauce in the freez-er for lazy, lonely evenings. All the recipes can be scale up or down; make sure your pan is big enough to cope with all the goodness.

HOW TO PAIR SAUCES & PASTA Choosing pasta sauces to go with your homemade pasta makes a big difference! Here, all the things to consider before assembly your signature dish. The dough, as both ingredients, flour, and egg, impact the texture, color, and taste of the pasta. As a general rule, more robust pasta stands up well to rustic and meaty sauces, while silky pasta pairs better with delicate and creamy sauces. Different combinations of flour and eggs open an array of many pasta possi-bilities and a bit of experimentation will help you to find the right mix!

The structure of the dough determines the shape of the pasta. Dough made with flour and water results a bit stiffer and works well with pasta with a more chewing consistency, like orecchiette and cavatelli. Flour and whole egg, the most traditional combina-tion, creates a softer dough that works for almost all pasta shapes. The yolk adds richness to the dough, thus flour and yolk for ravioli and long and flat noodles.

Flavours can be layered, paired, or highlighted and complex or simple dishes can be created.

As a general rule, flat and long pasta shapes go well with creamy sauces; long round pasta is the best for oil and tomato sauces as they coat each strand evenly. Flat and wide pasta like pappardelle as sop up the sauce better, go well with more substantial sauces like bolognese, porcini mushrooms, and rich tomato sauces. Thin, delicate stands like capellini and vermicelli (not mentioned here because they are not suitable for the machine) need light cream or oil-based sauces.

Concave shaped pasta pair well with chunkier sauces as they are ideal for capturing a variety of ingredients. Now let's distinguish between tubular and twisted pasta shapes. Large tubes go well with the bigger, chunkier sauce, while smaller tubes with finely diced ingredients. Both work well with stuffing and baking. Pair twisted pasta with finely chopped sauces, such as pesto and crumbled sau-sages. However, always consider how narrow or wide the curves are and bear in mind that the chunkiness of the sauce can vary upon your own taste. Filling pasta is already packed in flavored so, it is usually paired with light butter or oil-based sauces.

WHY CALORIES ARE NOT REPORTED Losing or gaining weight depends on your food intake and all the recipes in this book are made with fresh, healthy ingredients. The actual quality of the food is far more important than the actual number of calories! There are plenty of ingredients that are high in calories but super healthy, for example, banana, avocado, olive oil, and egg.

ESSENTIAL PASTA MAKING KIT Here, the complete kit to craft authentic Italian fresh pasta: rolling cutter, kitchen scale, pasta bite, bench scraper, wooden board, ra-violi try, stainless round cutter set or circular ravioli stamp, pasta stripper, sheet pans, parchment paper, spider strainer. Mallored-dus paddle and drying rack are optional.

TIMING We all like quick and easy recipes full of flavors, right?
Except when specified, the preparations and cooking time are the following:
• The dough preparation time is 40 minutes + resting time (30 to 60 minutes)
• Filling and saucing can often be prepared at the same time, while the dough is resting!
• Filling preparation time is from 5 to 40 minutes
• Sauces cooking time is from 5 to 30 minutes

ICON SET Suitable for lasagna and cannelloni. Leave the sauce or filling a bit more rough and add bechamel on top

 Vegeterian

 Super easy!

Tbsp: tablespoon
tbs: teaspoon

2. MASTERING THE DOUGH

Do you wonder why when googling "best recipes for homemade pasta" it is easier to get even more confused? Exists 600 different pasta out there, all with different shapes and consistency! Therefore, the perfect recipe for fresh pasta does not exist. The important thing is to understand the chemistry behind good fresh pasta and keep experimenting.

THE KEY ELEMENTS ARE ELASTICITY AND HUMIDIFICATION

When you knead the two main ingredients of dough-flour and moister (from the egg or water), they create a protein that gives pasta its structure and strength. The more your work the dough, the more elasticity you create. Do not worry to overwork your dough, it does not need to rise! In the case of gluten-free dough, a combination of xanthan gum, brown rice flour, and tapioca flour substitutes the standard network of proteins. The second factor is humidity. If the air is too dry, like during winter, the dough dries too quickly creating many empty holes between the flour and the pasta will result in brittle. So, during winter, add more water to the mixture. (Unless you can place a humidifier in the kitchen). On the other hand, when the humidity of the room is higher than the one of the dough, your pasta may result in a bit sticky. In this case, sprinkle some extra flour on the dough.

FLOUR

FLOUR 00 It is typically used by Italians for pasta making. Similar to All-Purpose, it is a soft wheat flour also perfect for baking. Double Zero means that the flour has been finely milled. Its powdery texture creates silky doughs that maintain their chewiness once the pasta is being cooked. It gives the pasta a nice texture and consistency and is lower in gluten than most American flours. It is not ideal for long soft pasta, it is perfect for ravioli. Typical fresh Italian-style pasta is made with Flour 00 and eggs.

> ### FLOUR & PROTEIN
> The protein content is very important because once the flour is mixed with the eggs, the proteins react giving straightness and consistency to the pasta. So, it is a good habit to check the nutritional information on the back when buying flour. Ideally, it should have between 10% and 12% of proteins; the lower the protein, the softer the texture. If you want to dry your fresh pasta then, you need high protein wheat, which helps to keep the shape once the pasta dries.

SEMOLINA A heartier coarse flour made from durum wheat, a hard type of wheat. It is darker and more golden than regular white flour. It has a rough consistency, a mild, earthy aroma and it is heather. It is low in fats but much richer in fiber and protein than regular flour. Semolina dough is a Southern Italian specialty and is made with Semolina and water only. It is easier to reserve because it is eggless. It is usually used to make dry pasta. For dry pasta, you will need high protein wheat which helps to keep the shape once dries.

BLEND For heartier shape and/or sauce mix 50% of Flour 00 and 50% of durum wheat flour. The mix makes the pasta a bit sturdier and helps the sauce stick to the pasta. The blend works very well for yolky dough, the pasta results with a delicate texture and the right amount of chewiness.

ALTERNATIVE FLOURS In addition to the classic Italian pasta-making flours (Flour 00 and Semolina), there are many other alternatives in the market.

Rye is vastly used, including in baking and brewing. Due to its high level of water, rye flour needs twice the amount of water. Rye flour leads to a rustic style of pasta. It works with long, short, and flat shapes and pairs magnificently well with green pesto and roasted cherry tomatoes!

Cornmeal pasta dough is rarely seen today but has its heritage in the north of Italy. The cornmeal adds a fantastic rustic texture that holds well the sauces. Pair well earthy sauce - truffle flavors, spicy meat sauces, and mushrooms. It is a very nice change for something a bit different.

NOT RECOMMENDED Farro has high protein content and it is low in gluten. It lead to a crumbly pasta dough. Spelt adds a sweet note to the pasta and leaves the texture a bit crumbled.

EGGS

> **BASIC EGG DOUGH THAT WORKS EVERY TIME**
> **1 LARGE EGG FOR 100GR OF FLOUR 00**

The eggs, besides providing moister, give fat which enriches the dough and provides a smooth and silky finish. The white and yolk have distinct nutritional facts and their ratio gives a different lev-el of silkiness and smoothness to the texture. Generally, the white allows more flexibility to the dough. While the yolk makes the pasta richer.

Most medium eggs are 55-65gr, the white part is 90%water and 10% protein while the yolk is 48% water and 17% protein, 33% fat and 2% carbohydrate.

When I knead, I usually make 3 meals for a family of 2 plus 1 kid. I like to keep two in the refrigerator for lazy evenings. You do not even have to defrost it before cooking it. Straight out of the freezer into boiling water. So handy!

If you may prefer to use less egg, substitute the eggs with warm water. Bear in mind that you need about 400ml of liquid (egg, water, puree) for every kilo of flour to get a rainy dough, neither too hard nor soft.

YOLKS Yolk adds color and flavor. A combination of whole egg and yolk makes the pasta richer and creamier.

EGGLESS ALTERNATIVE Ackee is a vegan alternative to eggs. Ackee is a plant that produces fruit and is considered a staple in the Caribbean diet. It can also be found in West Africa, Southern Florida, and Central America. Its fruits are very poisonous when unripe, while once they are ripe contain a good source of natural fat.
Ackee adds richness, a mild nutty flavor, and nutriment to a vegan pasta dough that, without eggs, would result in a bit flavorless. The dough is so packed with flavor that could be served with a drizzle of olive oil, sea salt, and black pepper, a light garlic sauce, or a sprinkle of cheese. It is also suitable for Ravioli or Lasagne.

OIL & SALT

Olive oil adds fat and flavor and makes it easier to work the dough. This is optional and completely up to you. I left it out from the rec-ipes, but feel free to give it a try. As a general rule, add ½ table-spoon of extra virgin olive oil to every cup of flour.

Adding salt to a dough slows down the formation of gluten, meaning that the pasta-making process takes longer. The dough needs to be kneaded longer to get the right consistency and texture from the gluten. This is the way Italians salt the pasta water instead of the dough.

MAKING THE DOUGH

INSTRUCTIONS
1. If you are making a small amount of pasta, it is better to knead the dough by hand. It is difficult for a food processor to mix well a small amount of pasta. I always give a bit of air to the flour before using it, the air incorporated into the mixture adds lightness.
2. Slowly pour the flour from one container to another one, as bartenders do with cocktails. But, it is not mandatory. Before starting with the flour, place a bowl of water nearby. You will need to wet your hands while working the dough. Sift the flour into a clean surface, give it the shape of a crater.
3. Add the whole eggs. With your fingers or with a fork, break the yolk and, with circulator movements, incorporates the flour into the eggs until the mixture comes together into a ball.
4. Now you can start kneading the dough with the heels of your hands, folding the mixture on itself and turning it a bit clockwise. And again, press with the heels of your hands, fold the dough and turn it clockwise. Keep doing this for at least 10/15 minutes. When the dough feels firm and a bit difficult to work but still smooth... you are done with the workout!
5. If you are working the mixture with a processor. Pour the flour and salt, let it run slowly for a couple of minutes (to add air), and then add the yolks (first) and eggs one at a time.
6. Keep the running slow otherwise, the machine will heat it and you will end up with beat eggs, rather than mix.
7. Wrap the dough with clean film or a dump cloth and let it rest for at least 1 hour before using it.

RESTING THE DOUGH During the resting time, the dough absorbs the humidity and the gluten relaxes. The dough will be stronger and easier to work. You can rest the dough for 30 to 60 minutes at room temperature cov-ered with a kitchen towel, up to 12 hours in the fridge wrapped in plastic film. Bear in mind that dough with high yolk content needs to rest longer.

CHAPTER 2. MASTERING THE DOUGH | 15

CHAPTER 2. MASTERING THE DOUGH | 17

TOP 5 TIPS
1. Use room temperature eggs
2. Do not add salt to the dough
3. Cook fresh pasta in a large amount of water for preventing the fresh or dry pasta from sticking together
4. Do not cover fresh pasta with plastic, it makes the pasta sticky
5. Even though it is almost impossible, be careful to do not over-knead the dough, your pasta can result chewy. If you overwork the dough, the mixture builds up so much elasticity that it is impossible to continue. However, if your dough results from a bit too hard or do not collect all the flour, add a tablespoon of warm water and continue to knead until the dough is smooth and firm

---

QUICK TROUBLESHOOTING

Tough dough: too much flour, gradually add water

Crumbly dough: add some water, a teaspoon at the time

Pasta not coming together: it needs more liquid

Dough tears when going through the rolling machine: if it's on the first pass it was probably too thick. Just keep folding it over, not too thick, and passing it through until it becomes smooth. If it tears after the kneading process, my best guess is that your dough is too wet. You need to add more flour so that it can pass through without sticking to the rollers. Trust me stick with it and it's a ton of fun.

Chewy pasta: not enough resting time allowed

3. DRY, COOK & STORE

HOW TO DRY FRESH PASTA Before cooking the fresh pasta, always let it dry for at least 30 minutes. This passage is extremely important for mainly two rea-sons: There are two main reasons why it is important to dry fresh pasta before cooking:

1. Become more firm and hold better the shape
2. Become less sticky, which prevents it from sticking together when is cooked

Remember to toss the pasta with a small amount of flour to avoid sticking. Then, hang the strands of pasta on a drying. If you do not have one, no problem! You can lay it well spaced on a baking sheet or a floured tea towel instead. You can leave the pasta out to dry for 4 to 6 hours turning it as necessary to dry thoroughly. To reduce the time, you can also use a food dehydrator. It takes 2 to 4 hours at 135°F. You can preserve dried fresh pasta for 2 to 6 months.

COOK FRESH HOMEMADE PASTA DOUGH So many foreigners cook pasta in warm water! Please, bring the water to a boil, add salt and throw the pasta. Stir it once or twice during the cooking time. Do not cover the pot.

I usually do not put any salt in my dough, but if you added it to yours, I would suggest reducing the salt in the water.

The cooking time of fresh and dry pasta varies depending on the variety and size. The only way to know if it is ready is to taste it. The pasta should not be soggy and floppy or hard in the middle. It should be firm to the bite, al dente. Fresh pasta is usually ready once it comes to the surface, which means that the center has reached the boiling point of water.

Keep a colander nearby; drain the pasta straight away. In the case of filled pasta, use a skimmer instead of a colander. Hold ¾ cup of pasta water on the side for better coating the pasta while mixing it with the sauce.

When the pasta is done with cooking, transfer it to the saucepan. Add a bit of pasta water and stir frequently over high heat for 2 to 5 minutes. It is ready when the water dissolves and the sauce is nice and smooth. Serve immediately with a drizzle of olive oil and fresh herbs.

---

4 LITERS FOR EVERY POUND OF PASTA
1 TO 2 TABLESPOONS OF SALT FOR EVERY POUND OF PASTA

REFRIGERATING & FREEZING Do not use any plastic; it will make the pasta sticky or it will stick to it.

You can place it in the refrigerator for maximum two days. Place it on a parchment-lined sheet pan with plenty of Semolina flour. Always slightly dry the fresh pasta before freezing it. Place it on a baking sheet, hung it to a drier rack or place it on a flowered tea towel for at least 15 minutes. Then portion the pasta in airtight glass containers or paper bags. You can freeze fresh pasta for 1 month.

4. PASTA SHEETER

The manual, old school pasta rolling maker, is the cheapest options on the market today. You can find it between 15$ to 90$, depending on brands, material, and features. It can be upgraded by buying more attachments or buying a motor over time. It is operated by a hand crack and requires four hands, one person to turn the handle while the other person handles the dough through the machine.
It is ideal for rolling out pasta and cutting it into shapes. A sheeter can also be used to also make tortillas, pizza and pies crust, Chinese dumplings, and many other types of doughs.

It is crazy that pasta makers do not have standards settings! Sometimes setting number 1 is the thinnest, and sometimes is the thicknesses. At the same time, the thickness setting could be 1/8" or 1/16", depending on the maker. It would be useful to start thinking small, medium, and thick. Doing so will be much easier to take inspiration from different cookbooks.

BEFORE STARTING...

1. Always keep the table floured, so the pasta does not stick
2. Keep the flour nearby, and every now and then, re-dust the dough
3. Make sure the dough rested for at least 20 minutes at room temperature before using it

MAKER MANTENAINCE

1. Not dishwasher safe!
2. Pasta maker usually comes in with their own brushes for dusting off little bits of dough
3. Try to keep all the machinery part dry otherwise, to avoid sickly bits of wet flower in corners and naughty points
4. A warm dump cloth nicely cleans it
5. Fully dry before storing or using again Lubricate periodically (once a year or after 50 uses) with light mineral oil the gears
6. Add a drop of oil in each corner of the rollers and cutters. hole to use the cut-ting roller or shape the pasta by hand

HOW TO ROLL THE PASTA SHEETS

1. Place the pasta machine on top of a towel and attach it to the edges of the table/surface by tightening the maker's clamp so that the machine does not bubble while rolling the pasta
2. Place the crank into the first hole – which is used to flatten the dough
3. Cut the dough in 4 pieces – keep one out and wrap them again the other three so that they do not dry out while you are working the first piece
4. Flat a bit with the palm of your hands and try to make it as rectangular as possible, so it will make it easier to roll
5. Flour a bit on both sides, so the dough does not get stacked into the maker
6. Make sure the rollers are at the wider setting – you can see they are pretty wide
7. Insert one of the shortest sides of the dough and start rolling, catch it from the other side
8. Fold the sheet in threes and flour a little more, pass it again from the shortest sides
9. Do it at least for three times – at the same setting
10. Progressively pass to a lower setting. Now you do not have to fold it into three each time. Just move the setting. Do not jump the setting; it does not speed up things, it tears the pasta.
11. When the sheet start to be a bit too long, cut it into half, so it is more manageable. Place one piece on the side and work on the other sheet
12. Pasta machines usually have 8 to 10 settings. I usually roll my pasta to the last setting. However, the thickness of the pasta depends on your own taste and/or the recipe requirements. Thin layers work better for ravioli, tagliatelle and linguine.
13. Once you have the sheet done, you decide what to do:
    - Trim the irregularity to make ravioli
    - Measure it to make lasagna
    - Cut them into fettuccine o linguine - Place the crank into the second hole to use the cutting roller or shape the pasta by hand

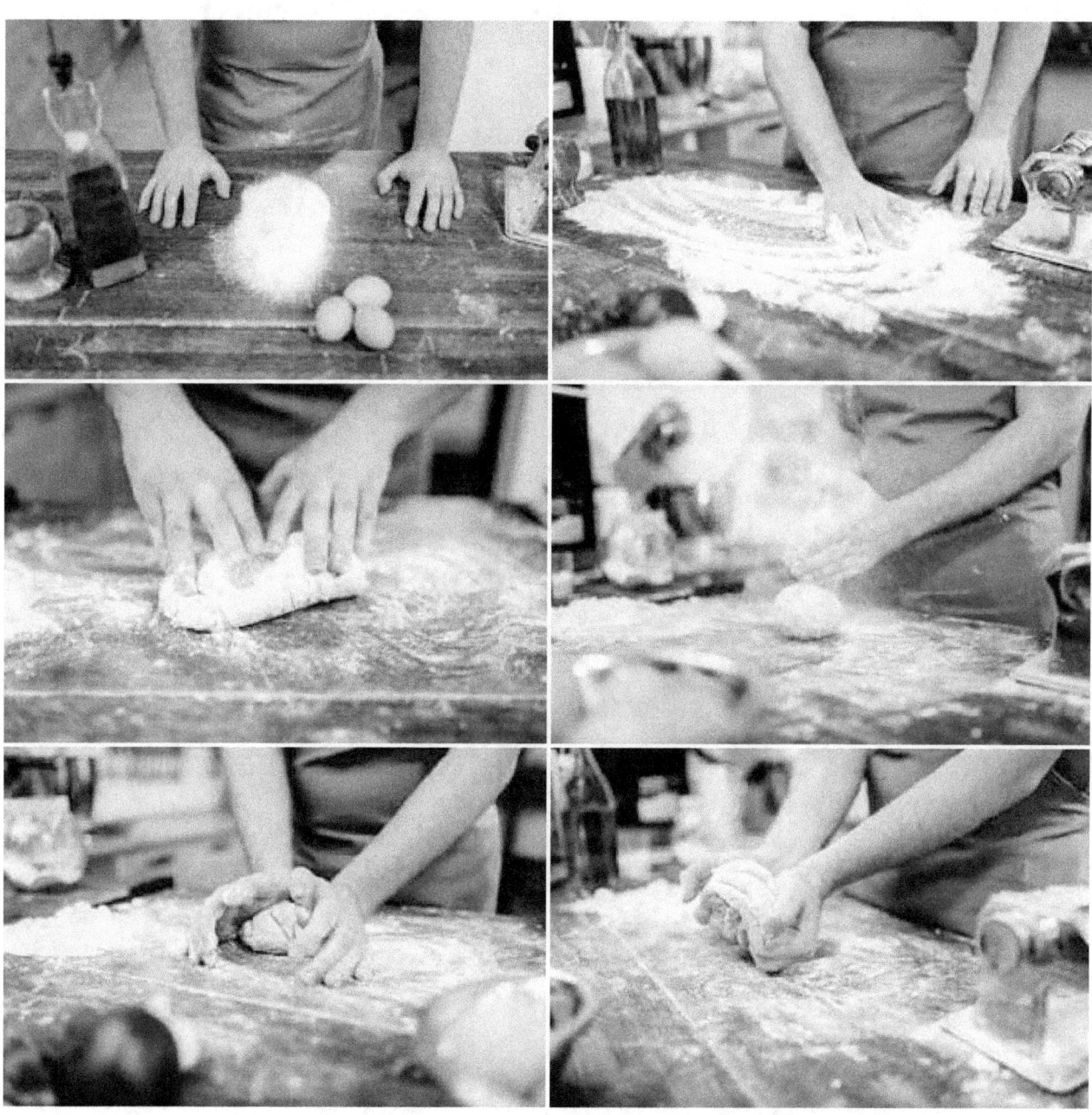

CHAPTER 4. PASTA SHEETER | 29

LASAGNE

Originally from Southern Italy, dating back to the 13th Century are one of the earliest types of pasta and their texture varies from region to region. With so many alternatives, it is really up to up! You can decide to knead a Semolina or egg dough, and also the thick-ness of the sheets depends on your own preference. Bear in mind that the thinness of the sheets enhances the flavors of the sauce. Traditionally the Semolina dough is used to make thicker sheets and serve with aubergine and mozzarella. Lasagne made with egg dough is usually served with bolognese sauce or meat ragu, Parmigiano, and bechamel. Egg and spinach dough layered with ham and cheese and covered with bechamel is another classic.

BECHAMEL

Lasagna needs Bechamel and a light or medium tomato-based sauce, depending on the main ingredients. The cream sauce keeps things moister and balances out the acidity of tomato sauce!
To keep it simple: vegetarian lasagna with light tomato sauce.
Meaty lasagna with medium tomato sauce.
Bechamel can also as a base for a rich, creamy cheese sauce.

INGREDIENTS

TIMING 5mns

For 1 cup of Bechamel (enough for an 8"x6" baking casserole)

2 Tbsp butter
2 Tbsp flour
1 ¼ cup whole milk
A pinch nutmeg
Seasoning to taste

INSTRUCTIONS

1. Melt the butter in a saucepan and add an equal amount of flour and cook for 1 minute
2. Add the seasoning and nutmeg.
3. Slowly stir the milk making sure that has no lumps
4. Bring the mix to boil, stir frequently until it thickened. About 2 minutes

INGREDIENTS	INSTRUCTIONS
400gr Flour 00 4 large eggs	1. Make and rest your dough (see Mastering the Dough) 2. First 3 to 4-time roll out the pasta sheets on number 6 or 7 on the dial 3. Roll out a couple of extra time on number 4 4. Pass the dough through again on number 2 or 3 for thinner results 5. If you are not using a machine, keep rolling out the dough until you almost see your fingers through the sheet 6. Cut the sheets into 4" x 5 ½" rectangles and let them dry on a drying rack or on a floured tea towel 7. Build the dish: layer the pasta sheets, sauce and cheese. Most lasagna have between 3 to 6 layers 8. Cook for about 35 to 45 minutes at 356°F (depending on the number of layers)

TOPS TIPS

- When completely dry, lasagna sheets can be store for up to one week
- You do not have to precook the fresh sheets before making the dish
- The number of sheets depends on their size and thickness
- With this recipes, you get about 500gr of lasagna sheets but, the number of sheets depends on the size and thickness you decide to go for
- You can also recipe to roll the sheets into cannelloni (filled with spinach and Ricotta, covered in bechamel and grated Parmesan on top)
- Make sure to use a pan that is big enough to hold all the good-ness in

CHAPTER 4. PASTA SHEETER | 33

TAGLIATELLE

Tagliatelle is long a flat ribbons from North of Italy, Emiglia Romagna. They are about 0.26" to 0.39" wide and the sheets are usually 0.30" thick but many variations spread around Italy. Tagliatelle is made with durum wheat Semolina egg dough and is traditionally served with meaty sauce. They can be served with more extravagant sauces creating a perfect marriage between traditional and modern cooking.

Tagliatelle and their many varieties work well with artichoke, broad beans, and peas, courgette and prawns, carbonara, ham, peas, and cream, saffron and langoustines, lemon and butter, oysters, Prosecco and tarragon, duck sauce, porcini, walnut sauce, truffle, rabbit and asparagus - lentils, smoked salmon, broccoli, braised bacon and peas - beef, veal or pork bolognese, tomato and basil, breadcrumbs and nuts.

VARIETIES OF THE SAME FAMILY

Tagliolini: long and cylindrical, made with egg pasta (0.35" thick / 0.8" wide). They cook very quickly and pair well with a light sauce and delicate condiments.

Bavette: thinner version.

Fettuccine: the typical Italian homemade pasta. Flat, narrower, and a bit thicker than tagliatelle. It is made with a traditional ratio of Flour 00 and egg (0.40" thick / 0.2" wide) and it is suitable for different preparations: meat, seafood, and vegetable.

Pappardelle: flat, large, and very broad egg pasta from Tuscany. (0.20" thick / ¾ to 1" wide). Rough to the touch and rich in flavor is usually pair with full-bodied condiments. pappardelle can be broken up into maltagliati.

INGREDIENTS	INSTRUCTIONS
3 cups Flour 00 3 eggs 1 yolk (optional)	1. Make and rest your dough 2. Cut the dough into equal parts and pass it through at the larger sitting 3. Fold it in half and pass through again at the large setting three times 4. Keep decreasing the setting and passing the dough through until the last setting 5. Attach the tagliatelle cutter and pass the dough through for the last time 6. Let them dry before cooking

TAGLIATELLE BY HAND First, flour the surface. Roll one longest side toward the center of the sheet and repeat on the other side and, without putting any pressure, fold it into two. Now with a shape knife, cut through the shortest side of your folded pasta sheet. Gently unravel the slices to reveal the ribbons (2" to 4"). Do not wait to do it; otherwise, all the layers will stick together. If you have a pasta drying rack, hung the tagliatelle to dry before cooking. Otherwise, you can arrange them into loose nests on a clean kitchen cloth and sprinkle over some Semolina.

PAPPARDELLE BY HAND You can make them in two ways. The first method is like described above, with the only difference of the cut, a bit wider (0.5" to 2"). The second method does not include the folding part. Simply, cut the sheet with a fluted pastry cutter – as straight as you can!

RAVIOLI

Ravioli are for creative pasta lovers as they are perfect for experimenting with new combinations of flavors. They are made by two thin squares of pasta pressed together with a filling wrapped in the middle. The filling and shape vary according to the regions, but the dough is always made with Flour 00. The dough has to be as delicate as possible to do not detract from the filling. The pasta sheet should be paper-thin, about 1/8" thick, and about 4 inches wide and rectangular. Usually, set 3 to 4 is fine for ravioli.

Ravioli and Tortelli work well with any buttered sauce, marjoram and toasted pine nuts, tomato sauce, walnut sauce, white truffle and porcini and cream.

INGREDIENTS

3 cups Flour 00
3 eggs

INSTRUCTIONS

1. Make and rest your dough (see Mastering the Dough)
2. Work your dough to paper-thin inches thickness

WITH RAVIOLI TABLET

1. Cut out sheets a couple of inches wider than your ravioli tablet
2. Add the filling and cover with another sheet
3. Place the cutter lid on top and add pressure with your body-weight to seal
4. Cut the ravioli in a single action

WITH RAVIOLI ATTACHMENT

1. Make your dough sheets of about 20" to 30" length and cut to the proper width
2. Flour the dough, fold it into two and insert it into the ravioli attachment
3. Crack the handle ¼ turn to introduce the sheet into the rollers
4. Open the sheets and add the filling – about 3 teaspoon
5. Turn the handle very slowly and keep adding filling as needed
6. When the entire sheet is being filled, let them dry on a floured tea towel and then separate them

VARIETIES OF THE SAME FAMILY

Tortelli: a square sheet of pasta, stuffed and folded diagonally to make a triangle. They have a hat-like shape similar to dumplings.

Tortellini: miniature Tortelli traditionally filled with veal or pork loin, prosciutto and Parmesan cheese and commonly eaten in a broth.

Mezzelune: circular or semi-circular Ravioli.

RAVIOLI BY HAND Cut your pasta dough into two equal sheets. Cover one of them with a cloth or clean film while you work with the first sheet. Add 1 tablespoon of filling raw and columns at 1 ½ " intervals. Lightly coat the remaining dough with beaten egg, you can use your fingers or pastry brush. The following step is a bit tricky... very carefully drape the other pasta sheet on top of the mounds. Press with your fingers between the pockets of filling to push out any trapped air. Now, cut the ravioli into squares. If you do not have a serrated ravioli cutter, you can use a sharp knife. Let it dry on a floured cloth for at least 60 minutes before cooking.

TORTELLI BY HAND On a floured surface, stamp out rounded shapes of pasta with a round cookie cutter. If you do not have one, you can use a small water glass with lightly dumped edges. Spoon your favorite filling in the middle and wet the edges with a beaten egg. Fold the edges into a crescent shape, gently press around the filling to push out all the trapped air. Bend the two corners in the middle to meet and press with your fingers to seal. Let it dry on a floured cloth for at least 30 minutes before cooking.

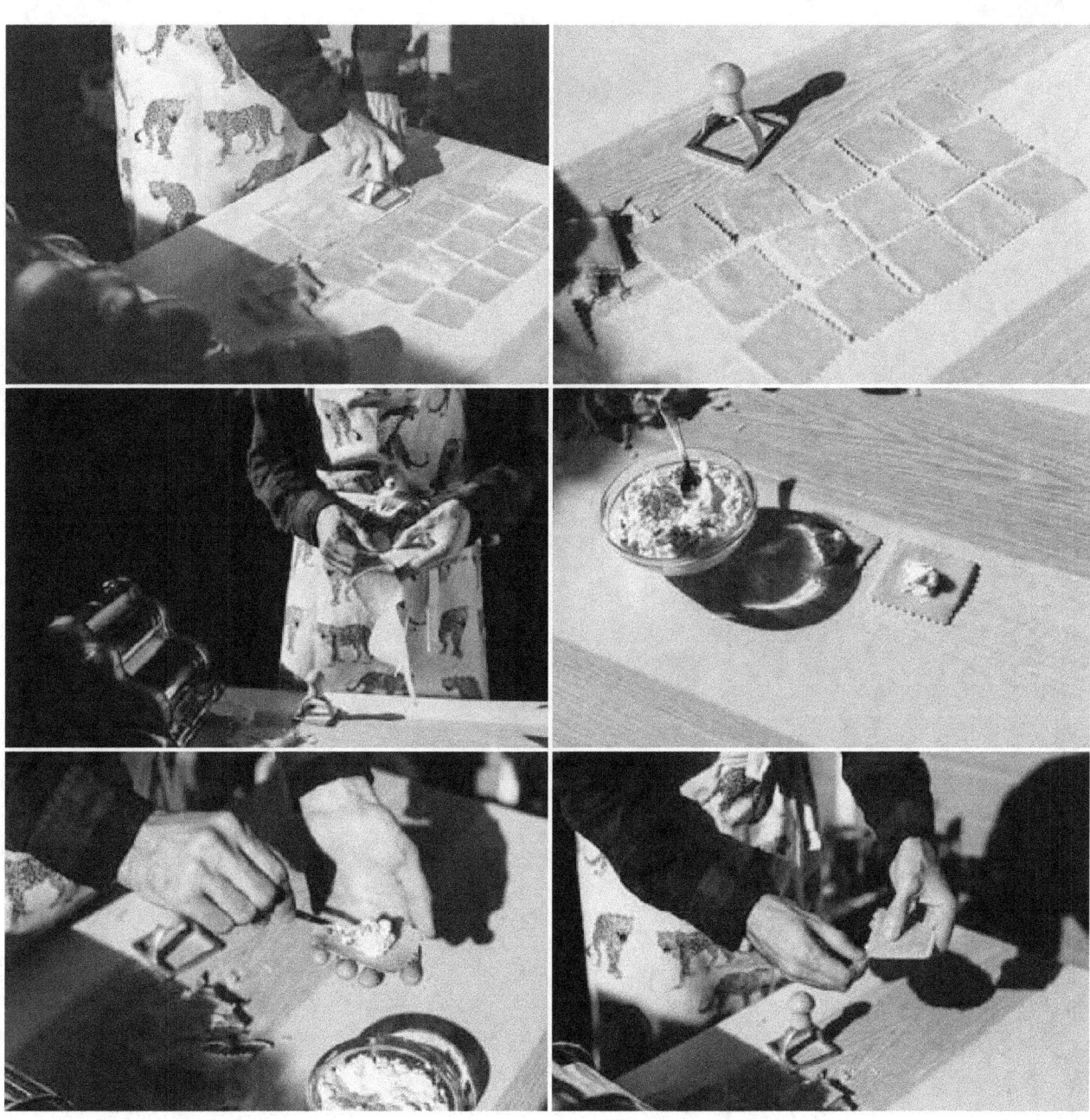

40 | PASTA MACHINE COOKBOOK

FARFALLE

INGREDIENTS

INGREDIENTS

3 cups Flour 00
3 eggs

INSTRUCTIONS

1. Make and rest your dough (see Mastering the Dough)
2. Cut the dough into three equal parts
3. Take one and cover the remaining dough to keep it from drying out
4. Flatten the dough with your hands and pass it through the largest setting of your sheeter. Fold it in half, rub it with more flour and pass it through the machine again. Keep folding the dough and passing it through the machine. Gradually decrease the setting until the second-to-last setting to make a long and thin sheet. You have to reach an even rectangular sheet of smooth, not sticky consistency
5. With a ravioli cutter trim off the edges and trim the rectangular into even strips, about ¾" wide. Then, cut the strips into 1 1/3" large pieces
6. With your fingers, push the side of each piece towards the center of the small rectangular
7. Secure the bow tie with a bit of water
8. Do not overlap the farfalle, sprinkle them with semolina and let them dry for about 30 minutes before cooking

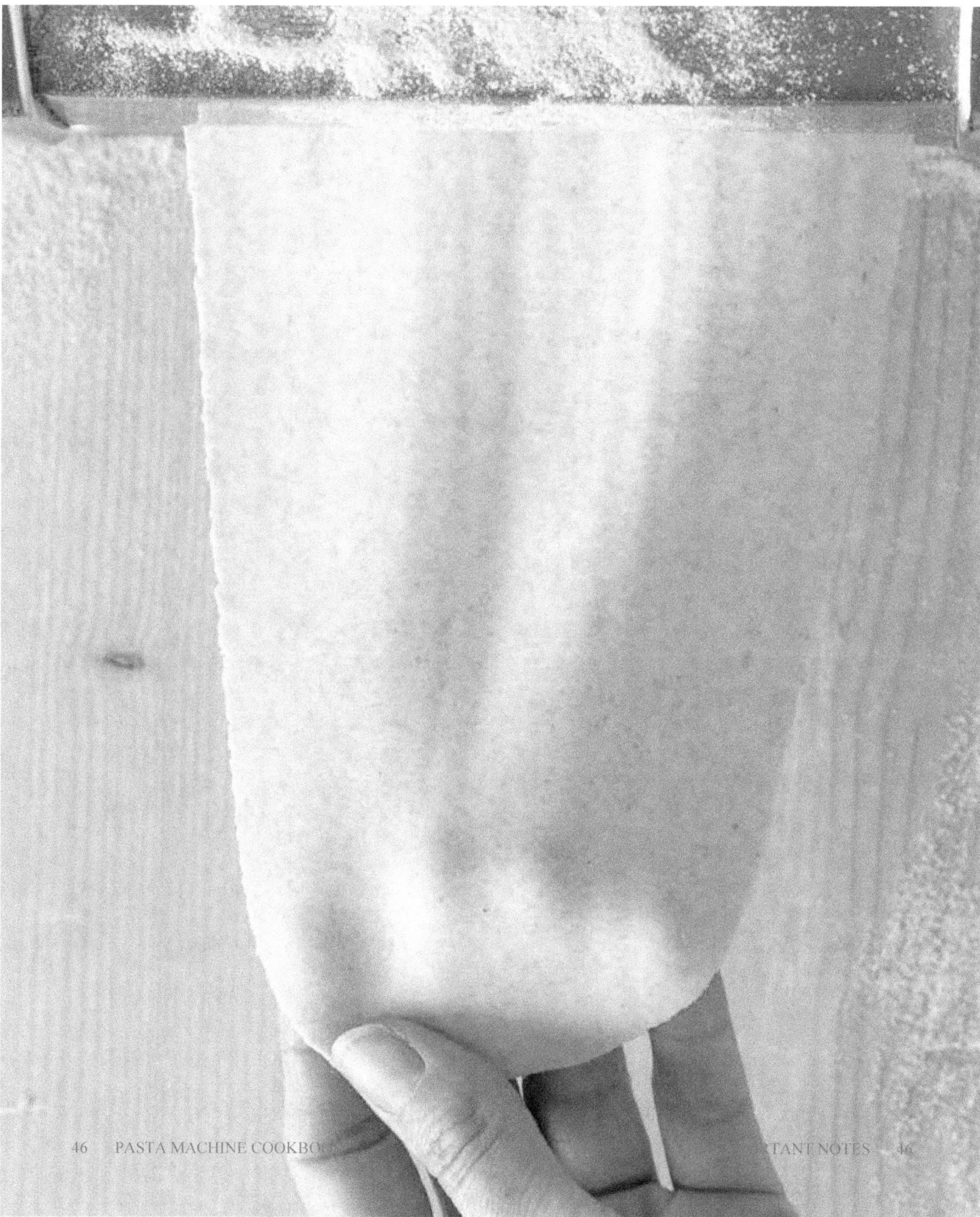

CHAPTER 4. PASTA SHEETER | 47

5. CAVATELLI MAKER

Cavatelli markers do not make the dough or sheets for you. First, you make the dough, cut pasta ribbons and then feed them through the machine while turning the hand crank. They are compatible with other attachments so, other kinds of pasta can be made, for example, Orecchiette and Gnochetti.

HOW TO USE A CAVATELLI MAKER

1. Make and rest your dough
2. Place the pasta machine on top of a towel and attach it to the edges of the table/surface by tightening the maker's clamp so that the machine does not bubble while rolling the pasta
3. Roll out the dough to 3/8" thickness
4. Cut the thick pasta sheet into ½" to ¾" wide stripes and roll each piece
5. Put the stands into the fluted cutter and manually roll the crack
6. Shape the pasta according to the cutter you have chosen

CAVATELLI

Cavatelli looks like mini hotdogs. The dough is quite thick and chewy and holds the sauces very well. It takes its name from its shape, the word Cavatelli derives from cavato, which means "carved." This classic Italian comfort food is so delicious that, even if it is not easy to make but, the hard work pays off!
Cavatelli is good with Cime di Rapa, broccoli, pork and pig sauces, pumpkin and goat cheese.

INGREDIENTS

4 cups Flour 00
1 ½ cups room temperature water

CAVATELLI BY HAND

Cut the dough into equal parts and make sure to cover the ones that you are not working on. Roll out your dough until you get a pasta sheet of medium thickness - about 1/6". Cut the dough into ribbons and then, cut each ribbon transversally to make 'mini hot dogs.' Each family like their Cavatelli at different length! I usually cut my dough into ¾" stripes and, each stripe into ¼" ½ " little piece. Now, it is time to carve the little pieces with your middle finger or thumb. Gently apply pressure in the middle with your middle and drag it towards you. Place them into a floured cloth and baking sheet, make sure that they do not touch each other. Promptly dust over some Semolina. The dough is very soft and they can easily stick together. Let it dry for at least 30 minutes before cooking.

ORECCHIETTE

They are made with Semolina and, widely eaten dry. However, fresh orecchiette are really good too!

They have the shape of a disk with thicker edges and a rough texture. Once cooked the center of the shape pushes out, becoming a perfect spot to catch the sauce. Also, the difference in thickness of the disk creates a fantastic contrast between the springy center and the thicker and firmer edge.

Orecchiette is good with Cime di Rapa and sausage, romanesco broccoli, lamb sauce, puree broad beans, green pesto.

INGREDIENTS

- 4 cups Semolina
- 1 ½ cups room temperature water

ORECCHIETTE BY HAND

Cut the dough into equal parts and make sure to cover the parts that you are not working on. Roll it out into long sausages and each sausage into smaller pieces. Now with a regular knife, press the dough down and, within one movement, slowly roll the piece toward you. With your thumb, unfurl the dough in the opposite direction to form that concave shape. Store them in a tray covered with Semolina while making the rest.

CHAPTER 5. CAVATELLI MAKER | 53

GNOCCHETTI SARDI

Gnocchetti was created in Sardinia, where they are called Malloreddus with means "little gnocchi" The semolina flour and the stripped shape give a unique scored texture and a pinch of saffron or turmeric in the dough (optional) adds a unique yellow color to the pasta. Gnocchetti is good with Sausage ragu, saffron, Pecorino, Ricotta, wild fennel.

INGREDIENTS

- 2 cups Semolina
- ½ cups room temperature water
- ¼ teaspoon ground turmeric or a pinch of saffron threads – optional

GNOCCHETTI SARDI BY HAND

Cut the dough into equal parts and make sure to cover the parts that you are not working on. Roll it out into sausages in length and each sausage into smaller pieces, 1" to 2" each as for Orecchiette. With your thumb, roll the dough over a gnocchi board or the back of a fork to create the ridges. The dough will curl and create a hollow center. Store them in a tray covered with Semolina while making the rest.

HOW TO COOK CAVATELLI, ORECCHIETTE AND GNOCCHETTI SARDI

They are done cooking when they float to the top; it usually takes 3 to 4 minutes. Overnight dried fresh pasta takes longer, 8 to 10 minutes. Freeze them for up to 3 months. When you take them out of the freezer, put them directly into salted boiling water.

6. EXTRUDER

Depending on the model, they can make different shapes of pasta (rounded, long, or both). Some work like the manual maker with a handle and a cutter, others are extruders; they simply push out a long straw of pasta that need to be cut by hand. The very basic version looks like a potato ricer and it can be found for just $19. Manual extruders work with a crank like a pasta sheeter and the basic version contains 5 dies. The price goes up to 300$ for pasta extruders that knead the dough for you and make the pasta in less than 15 minutes.

Electric Maker mixes the dough at the right consistency so that it can extrude the pasta smoothly but, the final pasta is consid-ered too smooth for many fresh pasta eaters and are a real pain to clean. Pasta extruder squeeze the dough out through the pasta dies, like toothpaste! Basically, the pasta is forced through a hole to make specific shapes like spaghetti, rigatoni, or other kinds of long and short pasta. The shape depends on the dies, which can be exchanged and an array of different pasta shapes can be created. The dough for the extruder needs a stronger structure to hold together tube-shaped pasta. First, you have to use Semolina flour in the flour mix. Do not try to substitute it with Flour 00– it won't work. Secondly, the dough has to be crumblier and dryer. Once the mixture goes through the auger, the texture changes completely, and the final pasta comes out of the right consistency, smooth and firm. Extruders tend to be quite slow, so I usually make a larger amount all at once, and then I freeze the restarting portions. Some people like to add eggs and to mix Semolina to Flour 00, I prefer the traditional recipes (without eggs). Here the ingredients for 21 oz. of pasta for both options.

TOP TIPS
1. Check the manual of your machine for the correct speed
2. The setting varies upon machines and pasta shapes
3. Short pasta length: 1" to 2"
4. Long pasta length: 10" to 11"
5. Dry the pasta 4 to 5 hours before cooking
6. You can refrigerate the pasta for up to 5 days
7. You can freeze up to 6 months
8. To clean the dies, dip them in water and then remove the softened leftover dough with a damp cloth

INGREDIENTS   INSTRUCTIONS

OPTION #1
NO EGGS
2 cup Semolina
¾ cup and 1 Tbsp of warm water

OPTION #2
WITH EGGS
2 cup Semolina
½ cup and 2 Tbsp of Flour 00
2 eggs

1. Mix the flour and water until the mixture has the consistency of damp sand
2. If it feels too wet, add more flour and vice versa
3. If you have an electric maker, screw in the desire dies to the extruder and put them on the attachment
4. If you have a manual extruder, place the pasta machine on top of a towel and attach it to the edges of the table/surface by tightening the maker's clamp so that the machine does not bubble while rolling the pasta
5. Grab about the size of a walnut of dough and put it into the hopper
6. Urge it toward the auger with a little shovel. Do not force loading the dough; when it makes contact, the auger will grab it
7. When you reach the length, you have to use the wire cutter or a sharp knife to cut the pasta
8. Sprinkle some flour over the pasta as it is done

SPAGHETTI

Spaghetti helped to spread around Italian culture, becoming the best-known pasta in the globe. A legend narrates that Marco Polo introduced pasta to Italy from the Far East in the 13th Century. So, there is a tiny possibility that spaghetti is likely to descend from Asian noodles.

What goes well with: anchovy sauce, carbonara, clams, prawns and zucchini, spicy garlic sauce, lentils, green pesto, ricotta and tomato, meaty sauces, cheesy sauces, broccoli, truffle, butter and Parmesan, mussels and ginger, salmon, creamy mushrooms... everything!

OTHER VARIETIES SIMILAR TO SPAGHETTI:

Bigoli: Thick spaghetti from Veneto. Quite rough, they easily absorb any condiments.
Capellini: They look like long filaments with 1mm diameter. They go well with light sauces.
Linguine: From Genoa. Similar to spaghetti but flat. Best combined with fresh and light sauces, seafood is the best combination.
Spaghetti Chitarra: Abruzzo. Similar to Tagliolini but thicker and square. Thick and meaty sauces.
Trenette: Typically from Liguria and served with pesto. Trenette has a square cross-section and a width similar to linguine. Light sauces.
Vermicelli: One of the oldest types of pasta, originally from Campania. Vermicelli has a round cross-section and 1 mm in diameter.

SPAGHETTI BY HAND Cut the dough into equal parts and make sure to cover the ones that you are not working on. Simply flatten the dough with your hand, do not worry about the thickness. With a sharp kitchen, knife cut out thin and long ribbon and sprinkle some semolina flour over your palms. Now, roll each ribbon between your hands, back and forward, until you achieve a thin circular ribbon. The diameter should be about ¼". Cut each circular ribbon at the desired length, 10" to 12". Do not overlap the spaghetti, sprinkle them with semolina and let them dry for about 30 minutes before cooking.

BUCATINI

The name Bucatini comes from buco, which means hole. Originally from Rome, it is a long pasta similar to Spaghetti. It is thicker and with a large cross-section which gives an interesting texture to better sop up the sauces. They get completely coated and filled with sauce! It is combined with strong and simple sauces.

What goes well with: Amatriciana - Anchovy sauce - cream and ham, pork - Ricotta and tomato - tuna and fresh cherry tomatoes - cacio e pepe - vegetable ragu - garlic butter sauce - pancetta and eggs.

CASARECCE

Typical short twisted pasta from Sicily perfect for chunky sauces as it perfectly holds sauces. With the rough surface and the iconic shape, Casarecce evokes the genuine pleasure of homemade pasta.

What goes well with: eggplant, Ricotta, and basil, braised bacon and peas, chicken and prune, Cime di Rapa and sausage, garlic sauce, rabbits and asparagus, courgette and pine nuts, sausage sauce, fresh tuna and cherry tomatoes.

> **CASARECCE BY HAND** Cut the dough into equal parts and make sure to cover the parts that you are not working on. Roll it out into long thin sausages. Then cut each sausage into smaller pieces, about 1" in length. With a barbecue stick, roll over the small dough to create a u-shaped cross-section and a slightly twisted shape. Store them in a tray covered with Semolina while making the rest.

MACARONI

Cylindrical curly pasta with a hollow and ribbed surface. With a small twisted shape and a rough and porous surface, it absorbs well sauced, adding a rich and strong taste. It goes well with rich sauces, especially meat and cheese.

FUSILLI

The curly spiral-shaped pasta from the south of Italy. The particular shape doesn't make them for holding sauces but, it holds a delightful mouth-feel. They work well with sauces, soups, cold salads, and casserole.

What goes well with: braised bacon and peas - fresh vegetable sauces - garlic sauce, lentils, Ricotta and tomato, lemon zest and pine nuts, simple tomato sauce, green pesto.

RIGATONI

Rigatoni has a cylindrical shape with a large diameter, a hollow, and a ribbed outer surface. This hearty pasta is great for baking pasta casserole as it absorbs well the condiment. Pair with substantial, punchy meaty sauces and with creamy or chunky sauces.
What goes well with: chicken and prunes, cream and prosciutto, garlic buttered sauces, meat and vegetable bolognese, Ricotta and tomato, sardines and fennel, sausage and mushroom, Pecorino and black pepper, pancetta and Pecorino.

PENNE

Another well-known pasta. It has a cylindrical shape and the ends are cut at 45 degrees. The texture can be smooth or ridged. The ridged ones are perfect for hearty, thick sauces like Bolognese as it captures more sauce.
What goes well with: chicken and prunes, fresh tuna and cherry tomatoes - cream and prosciutto, garlic buttered sauces, pesto - meat and vegetable bolognese, Ricotta and tomato, sardines and fennel, sausage and mushroom, Pecorino and black pepper, pancetta and Pecorino.

RECIPES

"Life is about exploring pasta-bilities"

(*) Quote from Internet

7. DOUGH

BASIC SEMOLINA • Ingredients: ¾ sup Semolina flour
　　　　　　　　　　¼ cup water

BASIC BLEND YOLK • Serving 6
　　　　　　　　• Ingredients: 1 ½ cups Flour 00
　　　　　　　　　　½ cup Semolina flour
　　　　　　　　　　2 large eggs
　　　　　　　　　　6 large yolks

RYE BLEND EGG • Ingredients: 1 cup Rye flour
　　　　　　　　　　½ cup Flour 00
　　　　　　　　　　1 large egg
　　　　　　　　　　¼ cup warm water

CHESTNUT DOUGH • Ingredients: 3 cups Flour 00
　　　　　　　　　　1 cup chestnut flour
　　　　　　　　　　1 cup of water
　　　　　　　　　　1 Tbsp of extra virgin olive oil

CORNMEAL BLEND YOLK
- Serving 6
- Ingredients: 4 large eggs
  3 large yolks
  3 cups Flour 00
  1 cup finely ground Cornmeal

SUPER CREAMY YOLK
- Ingredients: 1 cups Flour 00
  10 large yolks

ACKEE
- Ingredients: ¾ cup ackee
  1 ¼ cup Flour 00
  2 Tbsp spinach

CHICKPEA BLEND YOLK
- Ingredients: ¾ cup chickpea flour
  1 cup Flour 00
  3 large eggs
  1 Tbsp extra-virgin olive oil

Fresh vegetables and powder add colors and nutrients to your dish with very little effort (most of the time) and are a super quick variations of a basic egg dough.

TOMATO
- Follow the basic pasta dough recipes and instructions
- Add 2 tablespoons of store-bought or homemade tomato paste into the mixture

SAFFRON
- Follow the basic pasta dough recipes and instructions
- Soak 1 sachet of powdered saffron in 2 tablespoons of hot wa-ter for 15 minutes
- Drain the water and discard the solids
- Whisk the saffron water with the eggs before adding the flour

HERBS
- Follow the basic pasta dough recipes and instructions
- Add three tablespoons of finely chopped herbs to the flour

BLACK SQUID INK
- Follow the basic pasta dough recipes and instructions
- Add 1 sachet of squid ink into the eggs and whisk, before add-ing the flour
- You may need to add some extra flour to the dough as the ink makes it moister

PUMPKIN DOUGH

INGREDIENTS	INSTRUCTIONS
SERVING 6	1. Whisk the pumpkin and 1 egg in a small bowl
	2. In another bowl or a food processor, mix together Flour 00, Semolina, nutmeg, and salt
1/3 cup cooked pumpkin	3. Combine the two mixtures until they form one soft ball
2 extra-large eggs	4. Now add the second egg add pulse until the mixture forms small crumbs
2 ¼ cups Flour 00	
2 Tbsp semolina flour	5. Work the mixture until it forms a nice ball
Grated nutmeg	6. Sprinkle it with Semolina flour and knead with the heel of your hands for 10 minutes
1 tbs salt	7. Wrap it in clean film and let it rest
	8. Shape the pumpkin dough into any pasta!
TIP	If you hand up with some leftover pumpkin puree, you can add some sweetness to your next Mac-n-cheese
TOP PAIRING	Asparagus and crispy bacon sauce

SPINACH DOUGH

INGREDIENTS	INSTRUCTIONS
SERVING 4	1. Sauté the spinach with garlic and salt until cooked
	1. Place the spinach in a colander and press it with a fork to remove excess water
1 Tbsp olive oil	
½ cup frozen spinach	2. Make a puree with a food processor
	3. Make the dough by adding the spinach puree to the mixture at the very beginning of the process
1 clove garlic	
2 large eggs	4. Once the dough has form, knead for about 10 minutes, sprinkling with flour if necessary
1 large egg yolk	
2 cups of Flour 00	5. Wrap and rest the dough as usual for at least 30 minutes
1 pinch of salt	6. Shape the spinach dough into your desired pasta
TOP PAIRING	Ricotta and mozzarella filling

SWEET PASTA DOUGH

INGREDIENTS	INSTRUCTIONS
SERVING 6 TIMING 65mns 2 cups of Flour 00 ¾ cup sugar 2 eggs 1 stick butter – softened 1/8 pinch of salt ½ tbs active yeast Vegetable oil	1. In a bowl, beat the eggs, butter, salt, and yeast 2. In another bowl, mix flour and sugar 3. On a floured surface make the well and slowly add the wet mixture in the middle 4. With a fork and circular movements incorporate the flour into the eggs until you get a smooth ball 5. Work the dough a bit longer than usual - there is salt in the recipes! 6. Wrap it and let it rest for 1 hour 7. Make a paper-thin pasta sheet with the sheeter 8. Scoop in your favorite sweet filling 9. Add a couple of drops of vegetable oil to a frying pan 10. Cook the ravioli at medium heat until lightly brown on both sides 11. Sprinkle powdered sugar on top, enjoy!
TOP PAIRING	Nutella, homemade jam or peanut butter

SAFFRON & BLACK PEPPER

INGREDIENTS	INSTRUCTIONS
SERVING 4 3 cups of Flour 00 1 tbs black pepper ¼ tbs cayenne 1 tbs saffron threads ¼ tbs smoked paprika 3 large eggs 2 egg yolks	1. Combine Flour 00, salt, pepper, cayenne, saffron, and paprika 2. Follow the instructions for a basic egg dough 3. I recommend cutting it into linguine and serve it with a vegetable ragout
TOP PAIRING	Anything with sausage

FRESH CARROTS DOUGH

INGREDIENTS	INSTRUCTIONS
SERVING 6	1. Steam the carrots and make a puree
TIMING 60mns	2. Combine the puree with eggs and yolk in a mixer
	3. Add the flour and a pinch of salt and mix for about 20 seconds
4 medium carrots (to make about ½ cup of puree)	4. Knead the dough, wrap it and rest it for 1 to 2 hours
	5. Shape the dough into your desired pasta
2 large eggs	
2 ½ cups of Flour 00	
MY TOP PAIRING	Spicy lentil sauce

BEETROOT DOUGH

INGREDIENTS	INSTRUCTIONS
SERVING 6	1. Roast the beetroot with salt and olive oil for about 1 hour
TIMING 80mns	2. Let it cool
	3. Peel the beetroot and make a puree with a food processor
7oz beetroot	4. Make the dough by adding the beetroot puree to the mixture at the very beginning of the process
2 ¼ cups Flour 00	
1 egg	5. Once the dough has form, knead for about 10 minutes, sprinkling with flour if necessary
1 Tbsp olive oil	
2 cups of Flour 00	6. Wrap and rest the dough as usual for at least 30 minutes
1 tbs salt	7. Shape the spinach dough into your desired pasta
MY TOP PAIRING	Goat cheese and almons filling

EGGLESS WILD GARLIC DOUGH

INGREDIENTS | INSTRUCTIONS

SERVING 4
TIMING 60mns

250gr Flour 00
150gr wild garlic

1. Cook the garlic for 30 seconds - keep some water on the side
2. Make a pure in a food processor - add some leftover water if necessary
3. Squeeze out the liquid from the paste – now you should have around 120g of wild garlic puree
4. Now mix the puree with the flour and salt, follow the regular recipe to make the dough

MY TOP PAIRING: Rosemary butter and Parmesan cheese, chopped garlic on top

SAVORY CHOCOLATE DOUGH

INGREDIENTS | INSTRUCTIONS

SERVING 4 to 6

1 ¾ Flour 00
¼ cup cocoa powder, plus more for dusting
2 large eggs 1 Tbsp extra-virgin olive oil

1. Mix well the dry ingredients and make a well, proceed to make and knead until the dough comes together
2. Wrap it in clean film and let it rest for 30 minutes
3. Roll it out with the sheeter and cut into thin strips

MY TOP PAIRING: Tagliatelle, served it with a mushroom and rosemary sauce

ZEBRA DOUGH

INGREDIENTS

SERVING 4
TIMING 80mns

4 cups Flour 00
8 large eggs
4 packets squid ink

TOP PAIRING

INSTRUCTIONS

1. Make the regular dough using half of the flour and eggs. Rest for 30 minutes. Cut the dough into three equal parts and roll it through the sheeter as explained in *"How to roll your pasta sheet"*
2. Dust the sheets in flour and cover with a tea towel, set aside
3. Make the blank ink pasta using the remaining ingredients and rest for 20 minutes
4. Cut the dough into thirds and roll the pasta out in ½ inches rectangle. Pass it through the sheeter or use the fettuccine/noddle cutter
5. Run the pasta through to make colored ribbons
6. Floured them and put them aside on a tea towel
7. Now, place the plain pasta sheets on a floured surface
8. Make the colored pattern: place the black ribbon on top and gently press with a rolling pin
9. Carefully pass the zebra pasta through the sheeter until the desired thickness
10. Cut the pasta into the desired flat shape and add the desired filling
11. Fill with mint ravioli filling and served with light tarragon buttered sauce

Hot smoked salmon filling and three citrus brown butter

SWEET POTATO DOUGH

INGREDIENTS	INSTRUCTIONS
SERVING 6	1. Boil the potato for about 30 minutes until fork tender
	2. Mash them and set aside – you should get 1½ cup of mashed sweet potato
2 small peeled and diced sweet potato	3. In a bowl, mix beaten egg and sweet potato mash
3 eggs	4. Mix the flour and turmeric powder
3 cups Flour 00	5. Make the well with the flour, place the egg mixture in the middle and incorporate the two
1 tbs turmeric powder	6. Knead and work the dough as usual
TOP PAIRING	Smoked chorizo filling

RICOTTA DOUGH

INGREDIENTS	INSTRUCTIONS
SERVING 6	1. If you have a mixer, place all the ingredients in the bowl and set a medium speed. Otherwise, make a flour well and add all the ingredients in the middle
2 cups Flour 00	
2 cups Ricotta	2. Incorporate them and knead for 8 to 10 minutes until you get a smooth and elastic dough
1 egg	
4 Tbsp milk	3. Wrap the dough in clean film and let it rest for at least 30 minutes
MY TOP PAIRING	Cavatelli to go with and pair it with a broccoli rabe and broccoli sauce

STRAWBERRY DOUGH

INGREDIENTS	INSTRUCTIONS
SERVING 4	1. Blend the strawberries into a smooth puree, you should get ¾ cup of puree
12 fresh strawberries	2. Make the well on a floured surface
2 tablespoons water	3. Beat the eggs with the strawberry puree and then place the mix in the middle of the wall
2 ½ cup of Flour 00	4. Continue to work the ingredients as for a regular pasta dough; I recommend making ravioli, filled with Ricotta and mozzarella cheese
2 large eggs	
MY TOP PAIRING	Balsamic vinegar reduction, fresh basil and grated Parmesan cheese... you will definitely impress your guests!

TURMERIC DOUGH

INGREDIENTS	INSTRUCTIONS
SERVING 4	1. Mix all the dry ingredients together and follow the instructions for regular egg dough
4oz Flour 00	2. Once you get a smooth and little shiny dough, shape it into fettuccine, by hands or with the sheeter
4oz Semolina	
1 eggless	
2 yolks	
½ Tbsp ground turmeric powder	
2 Tbsp olive oil	
TOP PAIRING	Casarecce, serve with smoky apricot and chorizo bolognese

PORCINI DOUGH

INGREDIENTS	INSTRUCTIONS
SERVING 6 10oz Flour 00 0.7oz dried porcini mushrooms 4 large eggs 2 Tbsp olive oil	1. Put the dried mushrooms into a blender and run it until you get a fine power 2. Mix well all the dried ingredients and follow the instructions for basic pasta dough making 3. Wrap and let it rest for at least 30 minutes 4. Shape your favorite pasta
MY TOP PAIRING	Walnut sauce

WINE DOUGH

INGREDIENTS	INSTRUCTIONS
SERVING 4 1 1/4 cups Flour 00 1 medium egg ¾ cup red wine	1. Simply add the wine and egg in the middle of the flour and work as a normal pasta dough 2. Pair with butter or meaty sauces
MY TOP PAIRING	Caramelized figs and crispy prosciutto sauce

FRESH RED PEPPER DOUGH

INGREDIENTS	INSTRUCTIONS
SERVING 4 1 chopped red pepper bell 1 egg 1 ½ cup of Flour 00 1 Tbsp of olive oil	1. Blend the chopped red pepper bell into a smooth puree, you should get ¾ cup of puree 2. Add the puree to the dough when you break the eggs into the flour 3. Work the dough like a regular one
MY TOP PAIRING	Beef and mushrooms filling

BASIL AND GARLIC DOUGH

INGREDIENTS

SERVING 4
TIMING 40mns

2 large eggs
2 yolks
1 garlic clove
10 dried basil leaves
2 cups Flour 00

TOP PAIRING

INSTRUCTIONS

1. Blend the eggs, yolks, garlic, and basil
2. Add the mixture to the flour
3. Knead the dough

Serve with Pecorino sauce and fresh basil

SAUTÉ

It is a French cooking method adopted by their neighbors, which become the starting point of many Italian sauces and dishes. Sautéing means to cook in a small amount of oil or butter in a shallow pan over medium to high for a short time.
Sautéing browns the ingredients while preserving their texture, consistency, moister and flavor. In the case of meat or fish, the Sautéing usually finishes by deglazing the pan residue to make a sauce.

TOP THREE THINGS TO KEEP IN MIND:

1. The oil to lightly coat the surface of the pan is enough.
2. The ideal pan has to be wide enough to hold all the food in one layer and low edges.
3. The ingredients are usually put into small pieces and moved around the pan to speed up the cooking.

8. SAUCES

MUSHROOMS & ROSEMARY

INGREDIENTS	INSTRUCTIONS
TIMING 20mns	1. In a large frying pan, cook the mushrooms with the butter and seasoning until softened
2 Tbsp of butter ½ pound mixed wild mushrooms ½ cup heavy cream Splash of white wine 1 Tbsp minced fresh rosemary	2. Add the wine, turn up the heat and let the alcohol evaporates 3. Turn down the heat, stir in the cream and rosemary 4. Transfer the cooked pasta into the frying pan 5. Add 2 tablespoons of preserved cooking pasta water and toss well
TOP PAIRING	Pair with celeriac or potato filling

APRICOT & CHORIZO BOLOGNESE

INGREDIENTS	INSTRUCTIONS
TIMING 45mns	1. Dice the apricots into small pieces, mince the garlic and finely chop the onion
9 oz good quality Mexican Chorizo meat – uncooked sausage meat	2. Sauté the onion and garlic in a large frying pan until soften at low heat
2½oz dried apricots	3. Add the meat, apricots, oregano and chili flakes.
1-2 Tbsp chili flakes	4. Cook until the meat has browned at medium heat
3 garlic cloves	5. Add the freshly made pasta to the sauce and toss together
½ Tbsp of dried oregano	6. Served with chopped parsley on top
½ onion	7. Suitable of lasagna - cover with Bechamel sauce 1
Tbsp fresh parsley Seasoning	
MY TOP PAIRING	Orecchiette

SQUASH, GOAT CHEESE & WILD ROCKET

INGREDIENTS	INSTRUCTIONS
TIMING 45mns	1. Cook the squash in half of the butter over medium heat until golden brown
¼ cup butter	2. Add garlic, sage, lemon zest and fry for 1 minute
12oz peeled squash	3. Add the rest of the butter and a squeeze of lemon juice and fry until the butter melts
50 gr soft goat cheese	
2 chopped garlic cloves	4. Add the fresh pasta to the frying pan and toss well to combine
1 Tbsp lemon peel	
Handful wild rocket	5. Plate the pasta and crumble over the fresh goat cheese. Garnish with rocket leaves before serving
Handful fresh sage leaves	
MY TOP PAIRING	Pair with spinach and Ricotta filling

CREAMY TRUFFLED WILD MUSHROOMS

INGREDIENTS	INSTRUCTIONS
TIMING 30mns	1. Sauté the mushrooms and garlic, cook until they reduced size
6½oz mixed mushrooms – cleaned and peeled	2. Turn up the heat, add the wine and let the alcohol evaporates
1 minced garlic clove	3. Turn down the heat and add the dairy ingredients
2 Tbsp extra virgin olive oil	4. When the sauce has thickened, toss the pasta in
3 Tbsp dry white wine	5. Enjoy with fresh chopped parsley and a drizzle of truffle oil
¼ cup grated Parmesan cheese	6. Suitable of lasagna, cover with Bechamel
½ cup heavy cream,	
1 Tbsp fresh parsley	
Truffle oil (optional)	
1 knot of butter	
Seasoning	
MY TOP PAIRING	Chestnuts dough pappardelle or maltagliati

PECORINO SAUCE

INGREDIENTS	INSTRUCTIONS
TIMING 15mns	1. Place the dairy products into a small saucepan and cook over a bain-marie until the cheese is melted and warm
1¼ cup semi-cured Pecorino cheese	2. Add the nutmeg and salt, blend until smooth
¼ cup cream	
1 cup semi-skimmed milk	
1 pinch nutmeg	
1 pinch of salt	
MY TOP PAIRING	Carrots dough bigoli or farfalle

APPLE SAGE BROWN BUTTER

INGREDIENTS

TIMING 10mns

½ cup butter
16/18 fresh sage leaves
1 gala or honey crisp apple
1 Tbsp apple cider vinegar
¼ cup chopped walnuts

MY TOP PAIRING

INSTRUCTIONS

1. Toast the walnuts over medium heat – set aside
2. Peel, cored, and dice the apple
3. Melt the butter in a medium frying pan, add the apple and apple cider vinegar, and cook for about 2 to 3 minutes
4. Add the sage and cook for other 2 to 3 minutes
5. Transfer your fresh pasta to the frying pan and stir to coat
6. Serve with toasted crushed walnuts on top

Pair with spinach and Ricotta filling

BROWN BUTTER

Brown butter is what happens to the butter when you cook it long enough to melt it and develop a delicious toasty flavor but, not so long to burn it. It adds a rich and nutty flavor to your pasta dish and the combination of ingredients is endless. Sage, black truffle, lemon and garlic, rosemary, thyme... only to mention a few!

If you would like to thicken it a bit, add one or two Tbsp of cornstarch or Flour 00 to the cooking pan. Whisky at medium heat for about 3 minutes.

CITRUS BROWN BUTTON

INGREDIENTS	INSTRUCTIONS
TIMING 10mns	1. Prep the lemon and lime and set them aside
	2. Heat the butter until it starts to foam
¼ cup butter	3. When bubbling, add the shallot and swirl for 3 minutes
1/3 cup fresh orange juice – no beats	4. Add the orange juice and cook or other 1 minute
1 minced medium shallot	5. Add the fruit segments and stir until they break
½ lemon segments	6. Season to taste
½ lime segments	
Seasoning	

MY TOP PAIRING Pork, beef, raisin and Amarettti ravioli

GREEN OLIVES & BREADCRUMBS

INGREDIENTS	INSTRUCTIONS
TIMING 15mns	1. In a medium frying pan, golden the panko in a medium frying pan - about 5 minutes
1 Tbsp extra-virgin olive oil	2. Drain, season and toss with dill and lemon zest – set aside
¼ cup panko	
2 Tbsp chopped fresh dill	3. Mash the anchovies and garlic into a paste with a sharp knife
1 tbs finely chopped lemon zest	
4 anchovies fillets	4. Chop half of the olives and capers
1 small garlic clove	5. Combine with parsley, basil, olives, and capers (half chopped and half not)
1 cup chopped fresh parsley	
½ cup chopped fresh basil	6. Mix well and add extra virgin olive oil if necessary 1
cup pitted and halved green olives	
2 Tbsp drained capers	
2 Tbsp fresh lemon juice	
Seasoning	

MY TOP PAIRING Pair with garlicky dough

WILD BABY ASPARAGUS & CRISPY BACON

INGREDIENTS	INSTRUCTIONS
TIMING 30mns	1. Prepare the asparagus: remove the bottoms, cut off the tops and put them on the side, chop the remaining stalks
1 bunch of asparagus	2. Sauté the asparagus stalks in a large frying pan with olive oil and the pancetta until softens
12 thin sliced pancetta, sliced into small strips	3. Remove the heat and slightly mash them with a fork
½ cup grated Parmesan	4. Add the cooked pasta and toss well adding most of the Parmesan and black pepper
Seasoning to taste	5. Serve with grated Parmesan on top
Extra virgin olive oil	6. You can replace asparagus with peas if you like
MY TOP PAIRING	Chestnut dough

LEMON & PARMESAN

INGREDIENTS	Instructions
TIMING 10mns	1. Melt half of the butter, add the lemon slices, and cook for about 5 to 7 minutes.
8 Tbsp of unsalted butter	2. Stir frequently
1 small thinly sliced lemon	3. Remove the lemon slices and set them aside
1oz grated Parmesan	4. Scoop out a ½ cup of liquid for the cooking pasta and add it to the sauce
Seasoning to taste	5. Add remaining butter and whisk until you get a creamy texture
	6. Add the cooked fresh pasta and toss to coat
	7. Plate, add the grated Parmesan on top and garnish with the lemon slices
MY TOP PAIRING	Spinach and pecan filled pasta

CREAMY BUTTERNUT SQUASH CARBONARA

INGREDIENTS

TIMING 20mns

1 medium butternut squash
2 Tbsp extra virgin olive oil
2 egg yolk
4oz diced pancetta
1 minced garlic clove
1/3 cup grated Parmesan
Seasoning
1 tbs black pepper

MY TOP PAIRING

INSTRUCTIONS

1. Cut the butternut into half and remove the seeds. Roast it with a drizzle of olive oil for about 25 to 30 minutes – cut it into smaller pieces to reduce the timing
2. Mash the flesh with the yolks, a Tbsp of warm water, and seasoning – set aside
3. In the meantime, slightly fry the pancetta with the garlic until it gets crispy
4. Once the pasta is cooked, add the eggs and pancetta directly into the pasta pot and toss well. Cook for about 2 minutes (while mixing). Be careful to do not to overcook cooked it, you do not want pasta with scrambled eggs! It is ready as soon as the liquid of the sauce is been slightly absorbed
5. Spaghetti or bucatini is the best match, served with grated Parmesan and black pepper on top
6. For vegetarian options, remove the pancetta. Both alternatives work well with courgette as well. In this case, just pan-fried the courgette with garlic, when they are halfway through you add the pancetta

Bacatini or linguine

SPICY LENTILS SAUCE

INGREDIENTS | INSTRUCTIONS

TIMING 50mns

- 1 Tbsp light olive oil
- 1 finely chopped white onion
- 3 crushed garlic clove
- ¼ cup finely diced carrots
- ¼ cup diced tomatoes
- ½ cup dried red lentils
- 15oz can tomato sauce
- 2 cups of water
- ½ Tbsp red chili flakes
- 1 Tbsp chopped fresh basil
- 1 Tbsp dried oregano
- 2 Tbsp grated Parmesan cheese
- Seasoning

1. Simmer the lentils for about 15 minutes. Do not overcook them otherwise, your sauce will become mushy
2. When are done, remove the liquid and set it aside
3. Sauté carrots, garlic, and tomatoes with chili flakes and oil for about 3 to 5 minutes at medium heat
4. Add the tomato sauce, herbs and seasoning. Bring to boil and simmer over medium-low heat for 15 to 20 minutes, stir occasionally
5. Add the lentils and combine to the cooked pasta
6. Serve with grated Parmesan on top
7. Suitable of lasagna, cover with Bechamel sauce

MY TOP PAIRING: Chickpea dough maccheroni or fusilli

BROCCOLI, PEAS & PESTO

INGREDIENTS | INSTRUCTIONS

TIMING 30mns

- 14oz finely diced long-stemmed broccoli
- 7oz frozen sweet peas
- ½ finely chopped onion
- 8 Tbsp fresh basil pesto
- 2 Tbsp grated Parmesan cheese

1. In a large frying pan sauté the onion until softened, add the broccoli and cook for another 3 to 5 minutes. Add warm water if necessary to avoid sticking
2. Add the peas, cook over 2 minutes at medium heat
3. When the ravioli are ready coat them with pesto and add the vegetables and toss gently to combine
4. Pair with spinach and Ricotta filling
5. Serve with grated Parmesan on top
6. For lasagna or cannelloni add Bechamel sauce

MY TOP PAIRING: Cured ham and cheese mezzelune

CILANTRO & CHARD PESTO

INGREDIENTS | **INSTRUCTIONS**

TIMING 5mns

¼ cup cilantro leaves
1 ½ cup chopped chard leaves
5 slices sun-dried tomatoes, chopped
1/3 cup toasted pecans
½ cup grated Parmesan cheese
¼ Tbsp crushed red pepper flakes
3 clove garlic
Zest and juice of ½ lime
A drizzle of olive oil
Seasoning to taste

1. Place all the ingredients in a blender and blitz un-til you achieve the desired consistency. Done!

MY TOP PAIRING

Serve with gnochetti sardi or orechiette. Pair with smoked Chorizo filling

PESTO

The classic version of pesto is from Genoa (my home town!) and it is made with basil, garlic, pine nuts, Parmesan, and extra virgin olive oil. Today there are plenty of variations, from broccoli and broad beans, from arugula to watercress, from wild garlic to chive... and so on!

INGREDIENTS AUTENTIC PESTO

Basil
Nut
Olive oil
Garlic
Parmesan

Place everything in a blender and coat your pasta. You can store it in the refrigerator for about 3 to 5 days. But, if you cover it in extra virgin olive oil it will last up to a full week - Remove the top layer before using it.

HERE, MY FAVORITE VARIATIONS:

Watercress
Works well with whole-wheat pasta and courgette.
Add Brazilian nuts for a nuttier flavor

Chive
For a bit punchier flavor. Add a squeeze of lemon juice to balance out

Parsley
Swop pine nuts for hazelnuts for amazing flavors

Spinach
Mixed with walnuts. Add roasted cherry tomatoes as garnish

Arugula & Sweet Peas
Add pistachio instead of pine nut. Spicy and sweet bland

Kale
Superfood pesto that tastes good! Substitute the pine nuts with hemp seeds, toasted walnuts, or pecans

WHITE SAUSAGE

INGREDIENTS | INSTRUCTIONS

TIMING 30mns

7oz fresh sausage – casing off
1 thinly sliced onion
1 chopped carrot
1 chopped celery stick
1 tbs extra virgin olive oil
½ cup white wine
1 cup vegetable stock
1 rosemary sprig
1 thyme sprig
½ cup grated Parmesan cheese
Seasoning

1. Sauté the onions, carrot, and celery for about 4 minutes
2. Crumble the meat sausage and cook until white
3. Turn up the heat, add the wine and reduce
4. Turn down the heat, add seasoning, fresh herbs, and stock
5. Stir and simmer for about 15 to 20 minutes
6. Toss well with pasta and cheese
7. Pappardelle and orecchiette are recommended
8. Suitable of lasagna, cover with Bechamel sauce or tomato sauce

MY TOP PAIRING Tumeric pappardelle dough

WALNUT SAUCE

INGREDIENTS | INSTRUCTIONS

TIMING 10mns

1.2oz breadcrumbs
100ml whole milk
¾ cup toasted walnuts
½ garlic clove
2 Tbsp extra virgin olive oil
1 Tbsp fresh lemon juice
Seasoning
Chopped parsley and walnuts to garnish

1. Soak the bread in milk for a couple of minutes
2. Bland it with walnuts, olive oil and garlic into a paste - add a bit of milk to reach the desired consistency
3. Season and add a bit of lemon juice to taste

MY TOP PAIRING Cavatelli

SAFFRON & ZUCCHINI

INGREDIENTS	INSTRUCTIONS

TIMING 30mns

3 sliced medium zucchini
½ cup Philadelphia or cream cheese
1 Tbsp almond flakes
1 finely chopped garlic clove
1 bag saffron
½ cup chopped fresh parsley
Seasoning
1 tbs black pepper

1. Sauté the zucchini with garlic for about 15 to 20 minutes, add seasoning
2. If it gets too dry add a Tbsp of warm water to avoid sticking
3. In the meantime, toast the almonds flakes and leave them aside
4. Melt the saffron powder in 2 or 3 Tbsp of pasta water
5. Whisk cream cheese and saffron to get a nice creamy texture
6. Add the saffron cream, zucchini, and toasted almonds to the pasta pot when ready
7. Toss well to coat
8. Sprinkle a bit of black pepper and add fresh parsley on top

MY TOP PAIRING: Crab tortelli

TURNIP TOPS & ANCHOVIES

INGREDIENTS	INSTRUCTIONS

TIMING 30mns

2 cups turnip tops
1 sliced hot chili pepper
4 anchovies' fillets
1 garlic clove
Extra virgin olive oil
Seasoning

1. In a large frying pan gently fry the garlic clove and chili pepper
2. Add the anchovies, press them with a fork and let them dissolve a bit
3. Add the tops of the turnips and mix well to make a smooth sauce
4. Garnish with chili pepper rounds

MY TOP PAIRING: Celeriac and sage ravioli

ALLA NORMA

INGREDIENTS	INSTRUCTIONS
TIMING 35mns	1. Slice the eggplants about ½" thick and set aside
	2. Sauté the onions and garlic
1 large eggplant	3. Add the eggplants, seasoning and herbs. Stir frequently and cook in abundant oil for 5 to 10 minutes
Seasoning	
1 thinly sliced sweet onion	
3 crushed garlic cloves	4. Pour the crushed tomato in and simmer for about 15 minutes
28oz can crushed tomatoes	
¾ tbs dried oregano	5. When the pasta is cooked, transfer it to the saucepan and toss it well to combine with a Tbsp of pasta water
¼ cup chopped parsley	
¼ cup chopped basil	
½ cup grated Pecorino or Ricotta Salata or Parmesan cheese	6. Suitable of lasagna and cannelloni, cover with Bechamel sauce
MY TOP PAIRING	Short curved pasta. Grated cheese and fresh herbs

CARAMELIZED FIGS & CRISPY PROSCIUTTO

INGREDIENTS	INSTRUCTIONS
TIMING 20mns	1. Fry the prosciutto until the edges get a bit curly and set aside
4 thin sliced of prosciutto (cured ham)	2. Cut the figs into quarters and cook them in butter with the rosemary until they caramelized a bit
4 Tbsp unsalted butter	3. Stir occasionally until the butter brawn. About 3 to 5 minutes
6 fresh figs	
1 Tbsp chopped rosemary leaves	4. Add the cooked pasta to the pan, add the crumbled prosciutto and mix well to coat
Seasoning	5. Pair with cheesy or chicory filling
	6. The fried prosciutto adds saltiness to the dish so, season the water pasta a bit less than usual
MY TOP PAIRING	Gnocchetti sardi or chicory tortellini

CREAMY SUN-DRIED TOMATO

INGREDIENTS	INSTRUCTIONS
TIMING 15mns 2 Tbsp unsalted butter 3 minced cloves garlic 2 Tbsp Flour 00 1 cup chicken stock ½ cup heavy cream 1/3 cup drained and julienned sun-dried tomatoes in olive oil ¼ cup grated Parmesan cheese ¼ tbs dried oregano ¼ tbs dried basil ¼ tbs pepper flakes Seasoning	1. Sauté the garlic in butter 2. Whisk in the flour and stir well to remove all the lumps 3. Slowly add the stock, whisk for about 2 minutes 4. Add the cream, sun-dried tomatoes, Parmesan, herbs, and seasoning. Stir until slightly thickened
MY TOP PAIRING	Chestnut dough and garnish with parsley pesto

SWEET POTATO & MUSHROOMS SAUCE

INGREDIENTS	INSTRUCTIONS
TIMING 30mns 1 sweet potato ½ Tbsp olive oil 1 finely chopped small onion 4 chopped cloves garlic 1/2 cup cashews 1 tbs smoked paprika 9oz sliced mushrooms Seasoning	1. Boil the sweet potato until fork tender 2. Sauté mushrooms and 2 garlic cloves until they softened – set aside 3. In a separate fry pan sauté onion and 2 garlic cloves until slightly browned 4. Place all the ingredients (a part of the mushrooms) into a food processor and blend until you get a creamy texture 5. Combine the creamy sauce and the mushrooms in a frying pan, mix well over low heat 6. Add the cooked pasta to the pan to coat
MY TOP PAIRING	Mushrooms pappardelle

TOMATO SAUCE

Tomato sauce is a big deal for Italians and thus, it deserves its small own section. Three different tomato sauces enrich the pasta very differently.

LIGHT TOMATO SAUCE

Light tomato sauce has little body and creamy texture. It suits best delicate pasta shapes or filled pasta, such as spaghetti, ravioli, and light lasagna. The sauce itself is very fresh, light in texture and flavor. It is used in high proportion to the pasta. It is a great base for summery vegetable red sauces.

INGREDIENTS

SERVING 4 TO 6
1.4 lb. sauce

- I lbs. ripe vine tomatoes
- 3 minced garlic cloves
- 4 Tbsp extra virgin olive oil
- A small pinch of crushed chili flakes

INSTRUCTIONS

1. Cut the tomatoes in half and fry them with garlic, chili flakes, and salt over medium heat for about 20 minutes
2. While cooking, crush them with a fork
3. Add a bit of hot water when necessary to avoid sticking
4. Season with black pepper, extra virgin olive oil, and fresh basil leaves

MEDIUM TOMATO SAUCE

A good all-round sauce.

INGREDIENTS | INSTRUCTIONS

SERVING 4 TO 6
1.2 lb. sauce

3 minced garlic cloves
6 Tbsp extra virgin olive oil
a small pinch of crushed chili flakes
17oz ripe vine tomatoes
17oz tinned chopped and crushed tomatoes
½ tbs sea salt

1. Fry the garlic and add the chili, tomatoes and salt
2. Bring to boil and simmer for about 1 hour
3. Stir frequently and add warm water if necessary

RICH TOMATO SAUCE

The rich tomato sauce is clearly the opposite of the light version, reduced, oily, and concentrated. It is the perfect companion for the meaty sauce. A small amount of sauce is enough to coat long or caved pasta shapes.

INGREDIENTS | INSTRUCTIONS

SERVING 4 TO 6
1 lb. sauce

3 minced garlic cloves
6 Tbsp extra virgin olive oil
A pinch of crushed chili flakes
17oz ripe vine tomatoes
17oz tinned chopped and crushed tomatoes
½ tbs sea salt

1. Fry the garlic and add the chili, tomatoes, and salt
2. Bring to boil and simmer until the sauce is very thick and the oil has all risen to the top
3. Stir frequently an add warm water if necessary

9. FILLINGS

RICOTTA & SPINACH

INGREDIENTS	INSTRUCTIONS
TIMING 15mns	1. Wilt the spinach with garlic in a large frying pan over high heat
7oz fresh spinach 7oz Ricotta 1 ½oz grated Parmesan cheese 1 lemon A pinch of sea salt and black pepper 1 garlic clove	2. Remove the garlic and transfer the spinach into a colander and drain them 3. In a large bowl, combine spinach, Ricotta, a Tbsp of lemon zest, sea salt and black pepper 5. Suitable of lasagna and cannelloni, cover with Bechamel sauce or tomato sauce
TOP PAIRING	Serve Ricotta and spinach fresh pasta with sage, cheese and garlic butter

CELERIAC & SAGE

INGREDIENTS	INSTRUCTIONS
TIMING 10mns	1. Sauté onions and garlic in butter until they release fragrance
25gr unsalted butter 1 thinly sliced medium onion ½ thinly diced medium celeriac 2 thinly sliced garlic cloves 16 fresh sage leaves 250ml vegetable stock Seasoning	2. Add celeriac and sage and cook for 5 to 10 minutes at medium heat 3. Pour the stock and bring up to boil 4. Turn down the heat and cook until the celeriac is tender 5. Use a food processor to make a thick puree
MY TOP PAIRING	Pair with fresh kale, crumbled blue cheese and a drizzle of extra virgin olive oil (Add the kale to the pasta water a cook for just 1 – 2 minutes)

CLASSIC MEAT & CHEESE

INGREDIENTS	INSTRUCTIONS
TIMING 25mns	1. Fry the meat in olive oil until browned – dry with a paper towel
1 egg 1 Tbsp chopped fresh parsley 6oz ground beef 6oz pork sausage 8oz Ricotta cheese ½ cup grated Parmesan cheese 1 Tbsp extra virgin olive oil 1 Tbsp sea salt ½ cup spinach leaves	2. Mix all the other ingredients in a large bowl 3. Combine the two into a blender 4. Refrigerate the filling for at least 1 hour before using 5. Suitable of lasagna (do not blend) and cannelloni, Bechamel sauce
MY TOP PAIRING	Wine dough

CRAB

INSTRUCTIONS

TIMING 15mns

1/3 cup chopped red sweet pepper
¼ cup chopped onion
1 minced clove garlic
1 Tbsp butter
16oz can crabmeat
¼ tbs lemon peel
2 tbs drained capers
¼ tbs crushed fennel seeds
1/8 tbs black pepper

MY TOP PAIRING

1. Drain and flake the crabmeat removing the cartilage
2. Cook the sweet pepper, onion, and garlic in butter over medium heat for about 4 minutes
3. Stir in the crabmeat, lemon peel, capers, fennel seeds, a sprinkle of black pepper, and a squeeze of fresh lemon

Serve with a light citrus sauce and sprinkle over sliced green onions

RICOTTA & MOZZARELLA

INSTRUCTIONS

TIMING 5mns

8oz Ricotta cheese
2oz shredded mozzarella
2 garlic cloves – minced
A sprinkle of sea salt and black pepper

TOP PAIRING

1. In a large bowl stir together all the ingredients. Easy!

Green olives and breadcrumbs

ARTICHOKES & THYME

INGREDIENTS	INSTRUCTIONS
TIMING 45mns 2 globe artichokes 2 baby artichokes 1 lemon 2 shallots 2 garlic cloves 1 glass of white wine Parmesan cheese 1 spring of thyme 1 Tbsp of extra virgin olive oil A pinch of salt 2 cups of vegetable stock	1. Peel the globe artichokes and remove the center. Keep them in water with a squeeze of lemon juice until ready 2. Cut the baby artichokes into quarters and set them aside Sauté the shallots and garlic 3. Turn up the heat, add the white wine and let it evaporate, turn down the heat 4. Add the globe artichokes and vegetable stock. Put a lid and bring up to simmer 5. When cooked, leave them out to cool a bit 6. Finely chop them and place them into a food processor with Parmesan, thyme, a drizzle of olive oil, and salt. Blend until you get a smooth texture... done!
MY TOP PAIRING	Pair with Pecorino sauce

HOT SMOKED SALMON

INGREDIENTS	INSTRUCTIONS
TIMING 15mns 250gr hot-smoked salmon fillets 300gr Ricotta 2 Tbsp snipped fresh chives 3 Tbsp chopped fresh dill juice 1 lemon 25gr butter Seasoning	1. Place all the salmon fillets and Ricotta into a food processor and whizz well to combine 2. Transfer to a bowl, stir in all the herbs and lemon juice, and season to taste 3. Serve with dill butter sauce 4. Suitable for lasagna and cannelloni, cover with Bechamel sauce
MY TOP PAIRING	Serve with dill butter sauce

MUSHROOMS

INGREDIENTS	INSTRUCTIONS
TIMING 30mns	1. Sauté the shallots until golden brown in medium-size frying pans
17.5oz sliced chestnut mushrooms	2. Add the mushrooms and cook until they reduce in size
2 shallots	3. Add garlic and thyme and seasoning. Cook for a couple of minutes over medium heat
1 clove garlic	
1 Tbsp of fresh thyme	4. Let it cool for 5 minutes and transfer them into a food processor
1 heaped Tbsp Ricotta	
2 Tbsp grated Parmesan	5. Add the Ricotta and Parmesan cheese. Blitz until you get a smooth and thick puree
Seasoning	
1 Tbsp of olive oil	
MY TOP PAIRING	Asparagus and crispy bacon sauce

SWEET POTATO & GOAT CHEESE

INGREDIENTS	INSTRUCTIONS
TIMING 45mns	1. Wrap the sweet potatoes with garlic, olive oil, fresh thyme, and seasoning in aluminum
2 medium sweet potatoes	2. Roast at 350°F until the potatoes are soft – around 35 minutes
1 Tbsp of fresh thyme	
1 garlic clove	3. Remove the garlic clove and roughly mash the potatoes
2 Tbsp pumpkin seeds	
125gr crumbled goat cheese	4. Mix with goat cheese and pumpkin seeds
Seasoning	5. Suitable of lasagna and cannelloni, cover with Bechamel sauce
1 Tbsp of olive oil	
MY TOP PAIRING	Serve with a drizzle of chili oil and Parmesan or creamy sun dried tomatoe

SMOKED CHORIZO

INGREDIENTS	INSTRUCTIONS
TIMING 30mns	1. In a medium skillet cook the chorizo over medium heat for about 10 minutes. Let it cool
12oz chorizo, removed from casing	2. Mix chorizo, the three kinds of cheese, and the paprika to combine into a smooth and thick paste
4oz shredded mozzarella cheese	3. And your feeling is done!
1/2cup Ricotta cheese	
2oz crumbled feta cheese	
½ Tbsp of smoked paprika	
MY TOP PAIRING	Pair with cilantro and chard pesto

CINNAMON & PRUNE

INGREDIENTS	INSTRUCTIONS
TIMING 15mns	1. Boil the prune and fig until softened and chopped them in small pieces
250gr Ricotta cheese	2. Mix with Ricotta cheese and sugar
100gr prune	
1 dried fig	
1 spoon of sugar	
A pinch of sea salt	
1 Tbsp cinnamon	
MY TOP PAIRING	Dress your sweet cinnamon ravioli with melted butter, sugar, salt and cinnamon

PUMPKIN

INGREDIENTS	INSTRUCTIONS
TIMING 35mns	1. In half of the butter cook the onions and garlic until golden brown
1 small finely chopped onion	2. Add the pumpkin and the remaining butter, cook for about 10 minutes – Add hot water if necessary
2 Tbsp extra virgin olive oil	3. Pour the wine, increase the heat, and let the alcohol evaporates
50gr butter	
1 crushed garlic clove	
600gr peeled and diced pumpkin	4. Reduce the heat and keep on cooking the pumpkin until very tender
A small glass of white wine	5. Slightly mash the pumpkin with a fork. If you prefer a smoother consistency, blitz it for a couple of minutes
1 Tbsp fresh thyme	
½ tbs of nutmeg	
60gr grated Parmesan cheese	6. Combine with thyme, nutmeg, and Parmesan
MY TOP PAIRING	Pair with apple and buttered sage sauce

SAUSAGE

INGREDIENTS	INSTRUCTIONS
TIMING 40mns	1. With a sharp knife crumble the sausage as much as you can and cook it until white
4oz bulk Italian sausage	2. Add the spinach and stir well for a couple of minutes
¾ cup packed fresh spinach leaves	
1 egg yolk	3. The consistency of the mixture depends on your own preference. Leave it as it is or give it a blitz
1/3 cup Ricotta cheese	4. In the meantime, combine yolk, Ricotta, sage, and nutmeg in a large bowl
¼ tbs crushed dried sage	
1/8 tbs grated nutmeg	5. Stir in the sausage mixture
Seasoning	
MY TOP PAIRING	Wine dough served with broccoli rabe sauce

CURED HAM & CHEESE

INGREDIENTS	INSTRUCTIONS
TIMING 10mns	1. Mix well all the ingredients... done!
	2. Scoop the filling into your pasta sheet
5/8 cups chopped mozzarella	
¼ cup finely grated Pecorino cheese	
3/8 roughly chopped cured ham (preferably Parma ham)	
¼ cup chopped sun-blush tomatoes	
½ Tbsp chili flakes	
A handful of fresh basil	
Extra virgin olive oil for drizzling	
MY TOP PAIRING	Light butter sauce and freshly grated Parmesan

MINTY POTATO

INGREDIENTS	INSTRUCTIONS
TIMING 40mns	1. Boil the potato for 20 minutes until fork-tender
	2. In the meantime melt the butter with the sage leaves and let it cool
1 ¼ cups floury potatoes	
¼ cup finely chopped mint	3. Drain the potatoes and mash them with a fork
½ cup grated Parmesan cheese	4. Add Parmesan, mint, melted butter, and seasoning. Stir well to combine
Extra virgin olive oil	
Seasoning	5. Garnish with fresh mint and black pepper
3 Tbsp butter	
4 fresh sage leaves	
1 tbs black pepper	
MY TOP PAIRING	Serve with apple sage butter

RED ONION, BALSAMIC & POTATO

INGREDIENTS	INSTRUCTIONS
TIMING 40mns 2. 1 large Anya baking potato 2 large onions 1 cup balsamic vinegar 6 spring marjoram – leaves only ¾ cup unsalted butter ¼ cup grated Pecorino or Parmesan cheese 1 handful of rocket (optional) Seasoning	1. Boil the potato until fork-tender. Put aside In the meantime, cook the onion and balsamic at low-medium heat 3. Add half of the marjoram 4. Stir frequently to avoid sticking until the onion softened and the balsamic reduced 5. Mash the potatoes with a fork, grated cheese, the onion, and the pan juice. Season to taste 6. Combine with the balsamic reduction 7. Served the pasta with an herby butter sauce
MY TOP PAIRING	Try with strawberry dough and a dizzle of extra virgin!

GORGONZOLA & PEAR

INGREDIENTS	INSTRUCTIONS
TIMING 15mns 3 Tbsp butter 2 ripe pears 3 springs fresh thyme 7oz crumbled Gorgonzola cheese	1. Get your pears ready: peeled, cored, and cubed 2. Cook the pears with thymes in butter for about 10 minutes 3. Add the Gorgonzola and cook for others 2 to 3 minutes 4. Stir well and let it cool scoop the filling into pasta sheets
MY TOP PAIRING	Best served with walnut sauce

PORK, BEEF, RAISIN & AMARETTI

INGREDIENTS	INSTRUCTIONS
TIMING 25mns	1. Sauté the sausage meat until brown and add the minced beef
1 Tbsp unsalted butter	2. Cook for 3 to 4 minutes until the flavors combine
¾ cup crumbled sausage meat	3. Transfer to a large bowl and add the remaining ingredients
½ cup minced leftover roast beef	4. Mix well to combine
½ cup of bread crumbs	
2.4oz grated Parmesan	
3 crushed amaretti biscuits	
½ Tbsp soaked raisins	
1 medium egg	
Extra virgin olive oil	
Seasoning	
MY TOP PAIRING	Pair with asparagus and crispy bacon sauce, grated Parmesan cheese on top

LOBSTER

INGREDIENTS	INSTRUCTIONS
TIMING 10mns	1. Slice the tails into two and remove the meat, chop it and discard the shells
2 raw lobster tails	2. Combine with the other ingredients. Done!
8oz Ricotta cheese	
1 Tbsp chopped fresh chives	
½ lemon zest	
Seasoning	
MY TOP PAIRING	Serve with a citrusy light sauce

SPINACH & PECAN

INGREDIENTS

TIMING 10mns

½ cup chopped spinach
1 grated garlic clove
1 cup Ricotta cheese
¼ cup chopped pecans
¼ cup chopped red bell peppers
¼ Tbsp crushed red pepper
4 finely chopped basil leaves
½ Tbsp fresh thyme
Seasoning

MY TOP PAIRING

INSTRUCTIONS

1. Wilt the spinach and garlic for 3 to 5 minutes. Drain them well
2. Mix all the ingredients well...done!
3. Suitable for lasagna and cannelloni. Add Bechamel on top

Pair with carrot dough and light pesto

GOAT CHEESE & ALMONDS

INGREDIENTS

TIMING 10mns

8oz goat cheese
20 finely chopped fresh sage leaves
1 cup grated Parmesan cheese
½ Tbsp nutmeg
1 cup almonds
1 lemon, juiced and zest
¾ cup unsalted butter
Rosemary
Seasoning

MY TOP PAIRING

INSTRUCTIONS

1. In a large bowl, mix all the ingredients well. Done!
2. Serve with sage butter sauce and toasted crushed almonds, asparagus, and crispy bacon or broccoli, peas and pesto

Pair with beetroot dough

RICOTTA & MINT

INGREDIENTS	INSTRUCTIONS
TIMING 10mns	1. Mix all the ingredients into a food processor until you get a creamy texture
1 ¼ cups Ricotta ½ cup grated Parmesan cheese 1 Tbsp chopped ming 1 Tbsp chopped parsley 1 Tbsp chopped tarragon Extra virgin olive oil Seasoning	
MY TOP PAIRING	Pair with zebra dough and served with tarragon butter sauce

CHICORY

INGREDIENTS	INSTRUCTIONS
TIMING 20mns	1. Sauté the chicory leave and garlic until they soften a bit
¾ cup of finely chopped chicory leaves garlic clove 1oz Ricotta Extra virgin olive oil Seasoning	2. Drain before transferring into a large bowl 3. Combine with Ricotta and season to taste 1
MY TOP PAIRING	Pair with caramelized fig and crispy prosciutto or lemon butter sauce

PEACH & BASIL

INGREDIENTS	INSTRUCTIONS
TIMING 25mns	1. Cut the sausage into small pieces
	2. Cut the pieces into quarters, brush them with olive oil and place them on the grill until they get nice grill marks on both sides
6oz Ricotta cheese	
3 peaches	
½ cup fresh basil	3. Peel them and much them with a fork leaving it a bit chunky
4oz butter	
2 large eggs	4. Mix all the ingredients
¾ grated Parmesan cheese	
1 Tbsp extra virgin olive oil	
Seasoning	
MY TOP PAIRING	Pair with asparagus and crispy bacon, 3 citrus brown butter or caramelized figs and crispy prosciutto

BEEF & MUSHROOMS

INGREDIENTS	INSTRUCTIONS
TIMING 45mns	1. Sauté the onion until softened
	2. Add the beef to slightly brown
½ pound lean grounded beef	3. Add the mushroom and keep cooking until they reduced in size
3 ½ cups chopped mushrooms	
½ cup chopped onion	4. Pour the stock and simmer until it reduces. If it does not reduce, put the lid on and bring it to boil
½ tbs chopped garlic	
1/2 tbs basil	5. Let it cool and blend in a food processor with the other ingredients
½ tbs oregano	
½ cup beef stock	6. For lasagne and cannelloni leave the tiny chucks
1 Tbsp extra virgin olive oil	
Seasoning	
1 cup light tomato sauce	
MY TOP PAIRING	Pair with a light tomato sauce

TRADITIONAL GENOVESE

INGREDIENTS	INSTRUCTIONS
TIMING 45mns	1. Clean and boil the veggies for about 5 minutes, drain them well, and chopped them finely
10oz escarole	2. Soak the breadcrumbs in the stock for 2 minutes, drain them, and set them aside
7oz borages	
1 finely chopped medium onion	3. In a large frying pan, Sauté the onion and pine nuts until the onion softened
5oz veal	4. Add the meat and cook until browned
5oz pork	5. Drain the juice and combine it with the veggies, breadcrumbs, eggs, cheese, and herbs
5oz sausage	
1 Tbsp pine-nuts	6. Season to taste
2 Tbsp breadcrumbs	
¾ cup beef stock	
¼ cup grated Parmesan cheese	
3 eggs	
1 tbs finely minced marjoram leaved	
Nutmeg	
4 Tbsp extra virgin olive oil	
Seasoning	
MY TOP PAIRING	Serve with herby brown butter sauce or light tomato sauce

RICOTTA SUBSTITUTES

You probably have already noticed that Ricotta cheese is vastly used in Italian culinary tradition for its distinct sweetness and smooth texture. However, if you are looking to substitute with something else, here a list of suitable alternatives for pasta making.

GOAT CHEESE
It is the closest alternative to Ricotta. It is creamy and has a similar texture to Ricotta but it has a tangy flavor.

PARMESAN
It works best when mixed with other cheese like mozzarella and Bechamel sauce to bring out a similar Ricotta feeling adding salty and nutty flavors to the dish.

MOZZARELLA
A bit tricky. It has a similar sweetness but the texture is completely different. Mozzarella tends to be very stringy and clumpy so, you have to make sure you buy the creamier brand for good outcomes.

COTTAGE CHEESE
It is the closest alternative in flavor and texture. A good substitute if you want to go low-fat. It is dryer and firmer than Ricotta, to replicate Ricotta feeling you have to add moister to the dish. You can use cream to balance it out.

POT CHEESE
Possible alternative especially for stuffing and lasagna. It is dryer and firmer than Ricotta, to replicate Ricotta feeling you have to add moister to the dish. You can use cream to balance it out.

MASCARPONE
The distinctive flavors make it the perfect substitute for combatting strong garlicky flavors. It works in cannoli dishes. Due to its creamy consistency, you may need to blend it to make it a bit denser.

10. GLUTEN-FREE OPTIONS

The increased demand for gluten-free dishes brought many alternatives to Italian pas-ta, traditionally made with wheat flour. The alternatives range from black rice flour to quinoa and chickpeas. And, most of the recipes include xanthan gum, a common food additive used to add thickness and stability and prevent the ingredients to separate. Xanthan gum substitutes the gluten ensuring that the dough is flexible enough to be handled and shaped.

HOW TO COOK For perfect al dente pasta, you need to cook it for 3 to 4 minutes. **GLUTEN FREE** Gluten-free pasta tends to be starchier than wheat pasta. This **PASTA** means that when you add the pasta to the boiling water, an excess form may overload your pot. So, I suggest to use a big pot and fill it only with ¾ of water.

HOW TO STORE It is not recommended to preserve dried gluten-free pasta or **GLUTEN FREE** freeze the fresh one for a month as regular wheat pasta. Corn and **PASTA** rice flour tends to break down quicker than regular gluten pasta. It won't survive intact in the freezer or cabinet for a full month! I suggest to make and cook it as you enjoy a single meal. Even, cooking it a second time is a bit disappointing, you may end up with mushy pasta!

CHICKPEA
- Packed with proteins and fiber. It adds a light chickpea flavor to the pasta.
- Serving 4
- Ingredients: 4 Tbsp golden flaxseed meal
  ¾ cup warm water
  3 cup chickpea flour
  ½ cup tapioca flour
  2 tbs olive oil

CASSAVA
- Cassava flour is high in resistant starch which leads to many benefits for overall health. It is suitable for paleo diets.
- Serving 4
- Ingredients: 1 cup cassava flour
  2 large eggs
  2 Tbsp avocado oil
  2 Tbsp bone broth

QUINOA
- Quinoa flour is packed with vitamins, minerals, and proteins, healthy fats, and fibers. It is a good alternative for vegan and gluten-free pasta dough. Quinoa flour is less elastic than Sem-olina or Flour 00. If the dough is brittle, add a bit more arrow-root. Do not make the pasta too thin. If the dough cracks, add a bit of water to the crack with wet fingers.
- Serving 4
- Ingredients: 1 ¾ cups quinoa flour
  6 1/3 cups warm water
  5-6 Tbsp arrowroot powder
  2 Tbsp rapeseed oil
  ½ tbs nutmeg

RICE
- Serving 4
- Ingredients: 200g Rice flour or Cornflour
  100ml water or 2 large eggs
  2 Tbsp extra virgin olive oil
  2 Tbsp Xanthan

BUCKWHEAT
- Popular in Asian cuisine. But, we can use the Asian noodle recipes to make pappardelle or linguine!
- Serving 4
- Ingredients: 1 cup buckwheat flour
  2 large eggs

CHESTNUT
- Chestnut flour was vastly used in Italian culinary tradition as the flour of poor people and it was used to make a wide range of goodness from bread, porridge, cakes, biscuits, and pasta. Today is hard to find good quality chestnut flour and its price made it a real treat. It is a great alternative to grain it is very nutritious, riches in fibers, minerals, and vitamins. And it is perfect for making pasta thanks to its thickening properties. (See the Gluten-free pasta section for the gluten-free recipe). Its strong structure makes it especially suitable for long pasta. It goes well with walnut, butter, and sage, mushrooms, artichokes, pumping sauce, braised bacon, and peas. A bit out of topic but...sweet potato and chestnut gnocchi are a joy for your taste buds!
- Serving 4
- Ingredients: 2 ½ cup chestnut flour
  3 Tbsp tapioca starch
  3 Tbsp sweet rice flour
  ¾ tbs xanthan gum
  3 large eggs
  1 large yolk
  1 Tbsp extra virgin olive oil
  Water as need it

RECIPES INDEX

Ackee 64
Alla Norma Sauce 90
Apple Sage Brown Butter 80
Apricot & Chorizo Bolognese 78
Artichokes & Thyme Filling 99
Basic Blend Yolk 63
Basic Semolina 63
Basil And Garlic Dough 74
Bechamel 30
Beef & Mushrooms Filling 108
Beetroot Dough 68
Black Squid Ink Dough 64
Broccoli, Peas & Pesto 84
Brown Butter 80
Bucatini 59
Buckwheat Dough 115
Caramelized Figs & Crispy Prosciutto Sauce 90
Casarecce 59
Cassava Dough 114
Cavatelli 51
Celeriac & Sage Filling 96
Chestnut Dough 63
Chickpea Blend Yolk 64
Chickpea Dough 114
Chicory Filling 107
Cilantro & Chard Pesto 85
Cinnamon & Prune Filling 101
Citrus Brown Butter 81

Classic Meat & Cheese Filling 96
Cornmeal Blend Yolk 64
Crab Filling 97
Creamy Butternut Squash Carbonara Sauce 83
Creamy Sun-Dried Tomato Sauce 91
Creamy Truffled Wild Mushroom Sauce 79
Cured Ham & Cheese Filling 103
Eggless Wild Garlic Dough 69
Farfalle 45
Fresh Carrots Dough 68
Fresh Red Pepper Dough 73
Fusilli 59
Gnocchetti Sardi 54
Goat Cheese & Almonds Filling 106
Gorgonzola & Pear Filling 104
Green Olives &Breadcrumbs Sauce 81
Herbs Dough 64
Hot Smoked Salmon Filling 99
Lasagne 30
Lemon & Parmesan Sauce 82
Light Tomato Sauce 92
Lobster Filling 105
Macaroni 59
Medium Tomato Sauce 93
Minty Potato Filling 103
Mushroom & Rosemary Sauce 77
Mushrooms Filling 100

Orecchiette 52

Peach & Basil Filling 108

Pecorino Sauce 79

Penne 60

Pesto 87

Porcini Dough 73

Pork, Beef, Raisin & Amaretti Filling 105

Pumpkin Dough 66

Pumpkin Filling 102

Quinoa Dough 114

Ravioli 38

Red Onion, Balsamic & Potato Filling 104

Rice Dough 114

Rich Tomato Sauce 93

Ricotta & Mint Filling 107

Ricotta & Mozzarella Filling 97

Ricotta & Spinach Filling 95

Ricotta Dough 71

Ricotta Substitutes Filling 111

Rigatoni 60

Rye Blend Egg 63

Saffron & Black Pepper 67

Saffron & Zucchini Sauce 89

Saffron Dough 64

Sausage Filling 102

Sauté 75

Savory Chocolate Dough 69

Smoked Chorizo Filling 101

Spaghetti 57

Spicy Lentils Sauce 84

Spinach & Pecan Filling 106

Spinach Dough 66

Squash, Goat Cheese & Wild Rocket Sauce 78

Strawberry Dough 72

Super Creamy Yolk 64

Sweet Pasta Dough 67

Sweet Potato & Goat Cheese Filling 100

Sweet Potato & Mushrooms Sauce 91

Sweet Potato Dough 71

Tagliatelle 34

Tomato Dough 64

Traditional Genovese Filling 109

Turmeric Dough 72

Turnip Top & Anchovies Sauce 89

Walnut Sauce 88

White Sausage 88

Wild Baby Asparagus & Crispy Bacon Sauce 82

Wine Dough 73

Zebra Dough 70